the Ropes

▼ Second Edition

Knowing
the Ropes

▼ ▼ ▼ *Second Edition*

A Sailor's Guide to Selecting, Rigging, and Handling Lines Aboard

Roger C. Taylor
with illustrations by Kathy Bray

IM

International Marine
Camden, Maine

Published by International Marine

10 9 8 7 6 5 4 3 2 1

Library of Congress Cataloging-in-Publication Data
Taylor, Roger C.
    Knowing the ropes : a sailor's guide to selecting, rigging, and handling lines aboard / Roger C. Taylor : with illustrations by Kathy Bray. — 2nd Ed.
        p.   cm.
    Includes bibliographical references and index.
    ISBN 0-87742-391-1
    1. Knots and splices.   I. Title.
VM533. T39   1993
623.88'82—dc20   93-13540
                                                                        CIP

Questions regarding the content of this book should be addressed to:
International Marine, P.O. Box 220, Camden, ME 04843

Questions regarding the ordering of this book should be addressed to:
TAB Books, A Division of McGraw-Hill, Inc., Blue Ridge Summit, PA 17294
1-800-233-1128

This book is printed on 55-pound Glatfelter, an acid-free paper which contains 50 percent recycled waste paper (preconsumer) and 10 percent postconsumer waste paper.

Printed by R. R. Donnelley, Crawfordsville, IN
Design by Ann Aspell
Production and page layout by Janet Robbins
Edited by Jonathan Eaton and Pamela Benner

*I wrestled with intractable ropes, slaves if
they could be subdued, tyrants if they got
the upper hand.*

—Carruthers on board the

Dulcibella *in* The Riddle of the Sands

Contents

Acknowledgments

I've had a lot of help with this book. Particularly from Cynthia Bourgeault, who worried through the whole manuscript, rearranging things, and keeping me to the mark with both her judicious excisings and her urgings to explain further; and from Kathleen Carney, who insisted on clarity until she could do everything in the book based on the text alone.

Thanks, too, to Kathy Bray for her wonderful drawings, and to the staff at International Marine, my old home, for making it all happen.

Introduction

The purpose of this book is to present to the relatively inexperienced sailor practical, everyday ways of doing things with rope on a boat. By "sailor," I mean anyone who goes on the water, whether his or her vessel be propelled by sail or power. Because sails require so much rope and rigging, my emphasis necessarily will be on working with rope on a sailing boat, but the fact is much of what I discuss will be useful to the skippers and crews of powerboats.

We'll be looking at ropework and knots from the point of view of function: what are ropes for on a boat, and how do we make them work effectively and safely? Once function is determined and understood, then the kind and size of rope to use follows naturally, as do the method of rigging the rope and the best knots to use.

Rigging functions are basic and have remained the same since the earliest days of sail. Sailors have always needed a way to hoist and trim the sail, a way to keep the relatively stationary parts of the sail where they belong, and a way to secure the craft to an anchor or mooring point ashore. Some of these ways have hardly changed over the centuries, while others would seem strange indeed to a sailor from ancient times. The anchor rode is still in use, having merely become stronger for its size, more elastic, and smoother to handle. But metal fittings, some of them quite exotic, expensive, and difficult to repair, have by and large replaced the lashings that used to hold sails to their spars. Metal fittings, such as sail track and slides, can malfunction, so I will show you ways to replace them with rope if they do.

As a matter of fact, one objective of this book is to give you some alternative ways of rigging things on a boat, ways that are time-tested but are often overlooked in the general movement toward mechanization in order to ease physical labor. Sailboat rigs have become mechanized to some degree. I'm not thinking of high technology, of vessels whose sails are set or taken in by the push of a button, though this is becoming common among large, expensive yachts. Rather, I'm thinking merely of the winches that have replaced blocks, the wire that has replaced rope, and the metal fittings that have replaced lashings. There's nothing wrong with this mechanization; it works. It does change the ambiance of the boat from soft to hard; it introduces expense; it introduces reliance on the chandlery; and, strange to say, it sometimes increases the physical effort needed to sail the boat. In the last instance, I'm thinking of the difficulty, at times, of winching a straining line with no tackle as opposed to hauling on a line with a tackle. I don't expect all my readers to rush out and de-mechanize their boats, but I do want to present a few alternatives that you may find attractive, and that may—should a piece of mechanization fail—enable you to accomplish its function with rope.

We'll begin with a look at the basic kinds of rope and their advantages and disadvantages for various uses, followed by a brief review of rope terminology. Then I'll introduce the basic knots you really need on a boat and discuss their strong and weak points. I'll explain and Kathy Bray will show how to tie them. If you already know how to tie these knots—or can get a friend to show you—you won't need to read these necessarily verbose step-by-step instructions. The pictures are certainly worth more than the words, though the words are meant to clear up any mysteries or fill any gaps between the pictures. But that friendly teacher, showing you the knot by example, is usually worth more than both pictures and words together.

In the third part of the book, the real fun begins as we get down to the business of function. I'll describe good ways of handling lines—hauling, belaying, easing, coiling—because I have run across plenty of experienced sailors who unaccountably missed out on some of these fundamentals. I'll suggest ways of rigging halyards and downhauls, sheets and topping lifts, boom vangs and reefing lines. And I'll go into good ways to lash things down, tie things off, and generally rig things in a seamanlike manner.

Using the word "seamanlike" reminds me to say the obvious: this book is for women sailors as well as for men sailors, words like "seamanlike" or "seamanship" notwithstanding.

One of the marks of a good sailor is the way he or she uses rope. It is my purpose in this book to help you become a better practical sailor, marked by the way you use rope.

The Basics

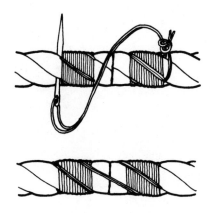

1 Properties of Rope

I just love going to the back of a chandlery and seeing all that new rope for sale. Knowing that you can never have too much rope around a boat, I'm always tempted to buy some just to have. You always use it, and nothing is more frustrating than figuring out a nice way of rigging something on your boat, say a down-guy to keep a poled-out jib from rising in a breeze, and then discovering that you don't have the right piece of rope for the job. You can visualize exactly the piece of line you need, but it's back in the chandlery.

So my first piece of advice about rope on a boat is: Have plenty of it, in assorted kinds and sizes.

Let's talk about some of the assorted kinds and sizes. The two basic elements of a piece of rope are the material it's made from and the way the material is formed into rope, or the way it is "laid up," as a ropemaker would say. Since this is a basic book, we'll cover basic materials and lay-ups only, leaving the high-tech, specialized ropes to more advanced studies.

The only materials we need to concern ourselves with are polyester (the best known of which is DuPont's Dacron) and nylon, plus a few words, chiefly of warning, about manila and polypropylene.

Polyester rope is wonderful stuff. It's strong, and it doesn't stretch much. It is resistant to chafing. It's relatively impervious to dampness, so it won't deteriorate when stowed away wet. It's smooth enough to be easy on your hands. It's good for any use on the boat. If you had nothing but polyester rope on your boat, you couldn't go wrong.

Nylon rope's chief value—and with it comes a specific danger—is its elasticity. (Nylon stretches about three times as much as polyester.) If you *want* a rope to stretch, then you want nylon. Many sailors prefer nylon for an anchor rode, because its elasticity will absorb any sudden jerks the boat might impart to the anchor. For the same reason, you sometimes see nylon dock lines. The danger is that if a nylon line should part under strain, all that energy stored

---

*A danger zone exists whenever nylon lines are under tension. In **A** the boat is kicking ahead against a forward spring to swing the stern out, preparatory to backing clear. When a towline is under heavy strain (**B**) the whole forward area of the boat becomes a danger zone.*

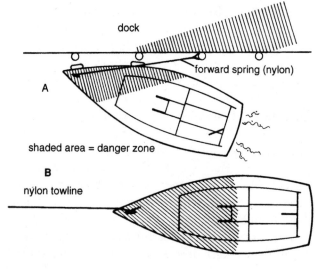

dock

forward spring (nylon)

A

shaded area = danger zone

B

nylon towline

up in the rope's elasticity will be released instantly in the form of the broken ends traveling along the direction of strain at literally lethal speeds. *A basic safety rule with any rope on a boat, but particularly with nylon, is: Visualize a straining line parting, and stay out of the line of fire.* Nylon is slightly stronger than polyester and is even smoother to handle; it's also impervious to dampness. It is not as resistant to chafe as is polyester.

For anchor rodes and dock lines, it's a toss-up between nylon and polyester. My own preference is for polyester. I'd rather give the anchor plenty of scope and double up the dock lines than depend on the elasticity of nylon to absorb the strain.

Before the invention of polyester and nylon, people had to use natural fibers for ropemaking. The most common ones were hemp and **manila**. Manila is still available, but compared to polyester, manila rope is weak, prone to chafe, and stretchy (though not elastic) under strain. It's rough on the hands, stiff when wet, and subject to rot if stowed wet. Even if not abused, it will not last nearly as long as polyester. Even an old purist like me has long ago given up manila.

Polypropylene rope is of interest only because it's so light that it floats, and because it is relatively cheap. It's prone to chafe and when chafed is particularly hard on the hands. Polypropylene's only conceivable use in a yacht is for a dinghy towline, where its floatability will keep it out of your propeller when backing down. But in that situation, the more seamanlike solution would be to have the dinghy either lashed alongside with a fender or snubbed up so short astern that her towline can't reach the propeller.

Rope made of any material will lose strength with age and use. Take good care of your rope. Keep it out of the sun all you can; keep it as clean as you can; keep it from

Cable-laid rope.

strand

yarns

fibers

chafing all you can. When your rope has been damaged by prolonged exposure to sunlight, by abrasion from grit, or by abrasion from chafing, replace it.

Rope is laid up in two basic ways: cable-laid and braided. **Cable-laid** rope is made by twisting fibers of Dacron, for instance, into yarns; then twisting yarns together to form strands; and, finally, twisting the strands together to form the rope.

Nearly all cable-laid rope is three-strand (you used to see an occasional piece of four-strand), and the strands are nearly always twisted together in the clockwise direction as you look at the end of the rope, thus forming *right-handed* rope. The rope is said to be *balanced* because the strands are laid clockwise; the yarns, counterclockwise; and the fibers, clockwise. Thus the elements support each other and tend to keep the parts from untwisting, or unlaying.

To make **braided** rope, fibers are twisted into yarns, and the yarns are laid next to each other—typically two, three, or four yarns—to form something comparable to a strand in cable-laid rope. These "strands" are then woven or braided into a pattern, either herringbone or diagonal checkerboard, to form the rope. The rope may be *single-braided*, with one weaving of the strands forming the entire construction, or *double-braided*, with a woven outer shell or cover tightly surrounding an inner core. The core within the shell may be of the same or different material.

Double-braided rope.

cable-laid core

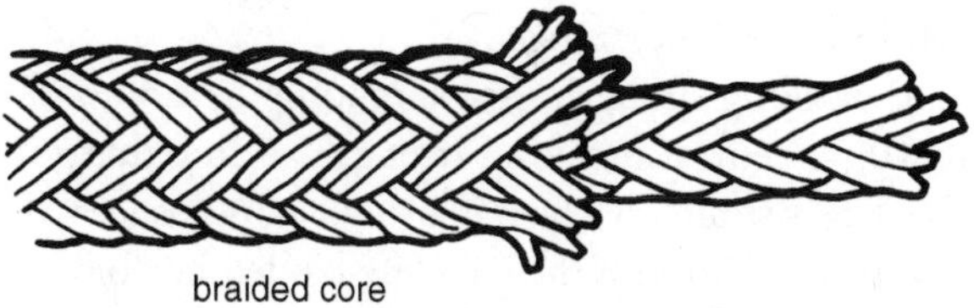

braided core

Usually the core of double-braided rope is also braided, but you sometimes find a braided shell over a cable-laid core, or even a plastic core.

Braided line, especially single-braided, should kink less than cable-laid, because there's no twisting involved in its makeup. (My own experience is that any kind of rope can kink up, but later I'll get into anti-kinking tricks.) Braided rope is usually slightly stronger than cable-laid, stretches a bit less, and is a bit easier on the hands. Thus, braided rope is ideal for sheets and halyards. On the other hand, braided rope is somewhat more prone to damage from chafe than cable-laid rope, so it's not as good a choice for anchor rodes.

My own preference is to use braided polyester for sheets and halyards, or any other line that will stretch a sail, such as downhauls, outhauls, and reefing lines, and cable-laid polyester for anchor rodes and for most other miscellaneous uses around the boat.

Braided rope is less supple than cable-laid, so it is harder to tie snug knots with braided rope, but the difference is not so great as to make you choose cable-laid over braided where braided is otherwise the better choice.

How big should rope be for a given use?

Today's polyester or nylon rope is very strong for its size. Quarter-inch rope has a breaking strength of nearly a ton; ⅜-inch rope, of nearly two tons; and ½-inch rope, of over three tons. These strengths are for cable-laid rope; braided rope is a bit stronger.

For working strength, you should figure on no more than 10 percent of breaking strength. A line that often takes a heavy strain on a boat is a single-part jibsheet when it is winched in to trim the sail close-hauled in a breeze. A formula for figuring the strain is $.005 \times A \times V^2$, where A is the area of the sail in square feet and V is the wind velocity in knots. Even for a modest jib of 200 square feet, the formula shows a strain of 400 pounds on the sheet in a 20-knot breeze, or 625 pounds in a 25-knot breeze. Say you want the sheet to be safe in a 40-knot breeze, even though you assume the sail will be safe in its bag if it's blowing that hard. That would mean you'd need a working strength of 1,600 pounds, calling for a breaking strength of at least eight tons. So you'd need ¾-inch double-braided polyester rope (though ⅝-inch would take you up to 37 knots without exceeding 10 percent of breaking strength).

In a small boat, where sails are small and strains on halyards and sheets are not great, you need only use small-diameter rope as far as strength is concerned. Yet any line that you are going to haul on with your hands ought to be no less than ⅜ inch in diameter, simply because anything smaller is hard to grip. And should you get mixed up in a ¼-inch line that comes under heavy strain for some reason, its small diameter can do some horrendous cutting that a bigger line wouldn't do. *Which brings up one of the oldest safety rules afloat: Never put any part of yourself inside a loop of rope.* (A corollary is: Never stand directly *on* a piece of rope.)

I happen to be writing this book while boatkeeping on board a well-rigged, 31-foot ketch. The sizes of her principal lines can serve as good examples for us.

The ketch's mainsail has an area of about 200 square feet; the mizzen has about 80 square feet; the working jib is about 200 square feet; and the big genoa, about 350 square feet. All her halyards are ⁷⁄₁₆-inch braided polyester, as is the mizzen sheet. The mainsheet is ½-inch braided polyester; it could be ⁷⁄₁₆ths also, as far as strength is concerned, but the ½-inch is just a little easier to grip and the mainsheet is a line you do handle a lot. The jibsheet is ⅝-inch braided polyester. Her anchor rodes are ¾-inch cable-laid polyester.

All good choices. None of this rope is in any danger of parting, and all of it is big enough to be easily handled.

Good rope is expensive. Because the safety of your vessel may ultimately depend on her rope, however, it is not wise to economize on rope. Select the best for the job, swallow hard, and buy it.

(Note: An outstanding source of detailed information on modern rope materials, construction, and size-and-type-for-various-uses is New England Ropes, 23 Pope's Island, New Bedford, Massachusetts 02740.)

2 Rope Terminology

Working with rope, like anything else, has its own language, so I'll define some of the terms I'll be using.

First is the familiar stickler about ropes and lines. The Old Salt asks you how many ropes there are in a ship, and you're supposed to say 700, or some big number, whereupon he smirks and says there are only seven: footrope, bell rope, wheel rope, and I forget the rest; all the others are lines. The point is that *rope* is the generic term, the stuff you buy at the chandlery, but when you start putting it to use on your boat, what you are rigging is a line with a specific name.

Here are the names of some lines and what they do. A *halyard* hoists and lowers a sail. A *sheet* trims the sail to the wind to best advantage. An *outhaul* stretches the foot of a sail out along a boom. A *downhaul* may haul down on the tack (forward, lower corner) of a sail to stretch its luff (leading edge) taut, or may be used to haul the sail down to hasten its lowering. An *earing* secures either the luff or leech (trailing edge) of a sail when the sail is reefed. Everything in this paragraph is *running rigging*, that is, rigging that moves (as opposed to *standing rigging*, which is rigging that holds fixed spars in place).

Dock lines secure a boat to a dock. They are, typically, a *bow line*, *stern line*, *forward spring*, *after spring*, and *breast line* as will be detailed later. A *painter* tethers a dinghy by her bow (she can also have a *stern line*); an anchor *rode* attaches a boat to her anchor. A *lanyard* is a short line used to hold part of the boat's rig in place. *Small stuff* is short lengths of small-sized rope that can be used, for instance, for various *lashings*, which are bindings to hold gear in place. One particular kind of small stuff is *marlin*, which is tarred for waterproofing and smells just wonderful. *Sail stops* hold furled sails in place. *Sail twine* is heavy thread, waxed to be water resistant.

In describing how a piece of rigging is arranged, I use the term *dead-end* to designate the point at which its fixed end is attached. I also use it as a verb, meaning to attach an end to a fixed point.

To *belay* a line, or *make fast* a line, is to secure it. Leading a line *to belay* means leading it to the cleat or bitt on which it will be secured. To *reeve* a line is to lead it through an *eye* (a circular fitting) or a *block* (a pulley). To

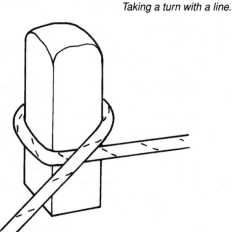

Taking a turn with a line.

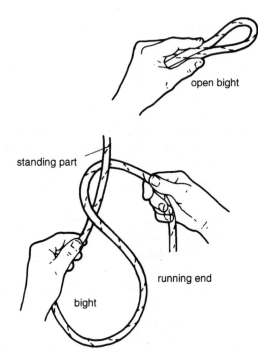

open bight

standing part

running end

bight

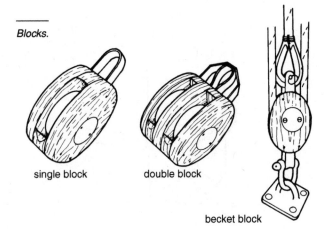

Blocks.

single block

double block

becket block

take a *turn* with a line is simply to wrap it once around a fitting, such as a cleat or post.

The end of a line is called its *bitter end.* The part used to make the knot is its *running end;* the main part around

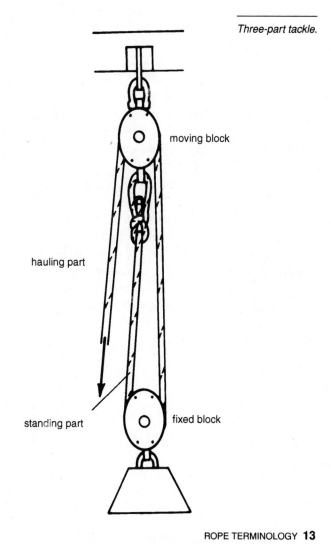

Three-part tackle.

moving block

hauling part

standing part

fixed block

which the knot is made is the *standing part*. A bend or loop in a line is called a *bight*. A line rove (past tense of reeve) through blocks forms a *tackle*. Each length of line in the tackle is called a *part*. The part that is dead-ended is called the *standing part*; the part you pull on is the *hauling part*, or *fall*. A *single* block has one sheave (wheel), a *double* block, two, and so forth. A *becket* block has an eye on one end to which a line may be dead-ended. A *cheek* block is one that is attached on the side of a spar. The more parts to a tackle, of course, the greater its mechanical advantage, on which more detail later.

In general, *knots* form fixed loops in the end of a line or tie the ends of a line together, *bends* tie the ends of two separate lines together, and *hitches* tie the end of a line to an object, such as an eye or a spar.

A *whipping* is a permanent wrapping of sail twine around the end of a piece of rope to keep it from unraveling. A *seizing* is a temporary wrapping of marlin or other small stuff around a rope to keep it from unraveling, or a wrapping of small stuff around two ropes to hold them together. A *serving* is a permanent, tight wrapping of marlin or other small stuff around a rope, wire, or splice to protect it. A *splice* is an interweaving of the strands of a rope to make a permanent loop in the end of a rope, or to join two ropes together.

3 The Ends of Your Rope

When you get out a piece of rope, whether new from the chandlery or old from your rope bag, to rig some line or other, you must concern yourself with the ends of your rope. We've seen how the parts of the rope were either twisted or woven together to form the rope; when you cut the rope to get the length of line you intend to rig, the ends made by the cut immediately start to unravel. Cable-laid rope will unravel, or unlay, more than will braided rope. Nylon cable-laid rope, in particular, will unlay rapidly when cut. Unlaid or frayed rope is lost to use, so we need to protect the newly cut ends of rope from coming loose.

With polyester or nylon rope, you can heat the ends with a match or cigarette lighter to "weld" the fibers together. (Usually, when you buy polyester or nylon rope at the chandlery, your piece will be cut off with an electric hot knife that welds as it cuts.) Or, you can wrap a narrow piece of tape twice round the end of the rope to keep it from coming unlaid. But these methods are not very strong or durable. The more seamanlike solution is to put on a sewn whipping.

A sewn whipping is a very tight wrapping of sail twine around the rope right near its end, about as wide as the rope is thick, held securely to the rope by binding stitches.

Sailor's needles and palm.

palm

round needles go through rope more easily

Once you get in practice, you can sew a whipping almost as quickly as you can singe or tape.

For whipping, you'll need a needle big enough to take sail twine through its eye and strong enough to stand some fairly hard pulling and shoving. Household needles are generally too small; you'll need a sail needle from the chandlery. Most sail needles are triangular in midsection. These work all right in rope, but for whipping, try to get a needle that is round in section, because it will go through tightly laid or braided rope more easily. For your final stitches, you may also need a sailor's palm, a heavy thimble embedded in a stout leather strap worn over the hand to let you push a needle with the strength of your arm.

Here's a good way to sew a whipping. Start by taking a length of sail twine of medium thickness. Trial and error will tell you how much, but generally speaking, one whipping on ½-inch rope requires a doubled length of twine about two feet long—or four feet of twine altogether (you'll be working with the twine doubled). Bigger or smaller rope obviously requires a bit more or a bit less. Overestimate when you start out—it's rather frustrating to be almost through sewing a whipping only to find you don't have quite enough twine on your needle. If the twine isn't already waxed, wax it. The wax is for waterproofing, hence durability.

When threading the needle, it often helps to flatten out the end of the twine with your teeth or thumbnail. Pull the twine through the needle until the ends are exactly even.

At this point you'll have to decide precisely where on the rope to place the whipping. If you're binding the end

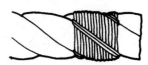

Sewing a whipping.

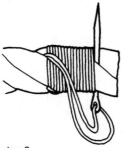

step 1

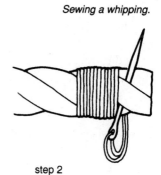

step 2

step 3

step 4

of a piece of rope, start the whipping where the rope is still firmly laid up, an inch or two from where the rope is starting to come unlaid. Don't be too stingy. It's better to waste a little solid rope than to put a whipping on rope that's already coming unlaid. Such a whipping won't hold.

Plan the width of the whipping to be equal to the diameter of the rope. Start the whipping about two diameters of the rope from the end, and wrap toward the end of the rope. On cable-laid rope, start by sewing under any strand where you want the starting edge of your whipping to be. Pull the twine through until the two ends are just left showing. With the thumb that is not holding the needle, smooth down these short ends of twine into the *contline* (gutter) between two strands of the rope, headed toward the end of the rope to place them under your whipping.

Start wrapping turns of the doubled twine tightly around the rope, working toward the end of the rope (covering the short ends left showing), taking care not to twist the doubled twine (untwist it by twirling the needle as

---

Finish detail for a whipping.

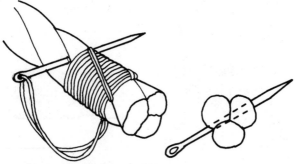

needle goes directly through rope

necessary as you go). Lay each turn in snug against the preceding one, and pull it tight. Keep wrapping until the width of the whipping is equal to the diameter of the rope. Then, holding the last turn you wrapped snug with that non-needle-hand thumb, sew through under one strand of the rope and pull *really* taut.

Now, take the twine diagonally back over the turns of the whipping along the contline between the strands of the rope (less visible under the wraps, but still discernible). Making sure the twine isn't twisted, sew through under one strand tight up against the first turn of the whipping. Next, come back diagonally across the turns of the whipping along the next contline (still making sure the twine isn't twisted), and again sew through under one strand of the rope tight against the last turn of the whipping. Repeat once more, going back across the whipping in the third and last contline available between strands, and sew through again, but this time, instead of sewing under one strand, sew directly through the rope so the needle comes out through the middle of the strand opposite. This gives the whipping a bit of extra strength. You may need your sailor palm to shove the needle through this last time, because it is going through a strand rather than under a strand. Note that by initially wrapping the turns of the whipping toward the end of the rope, you make the last strong stitch that goes directly through the rope on the side of the whipping *away* from the end of the rope. This makes the whipping stronger than if you'd done it the other way around.

Now cut the twine off flush with the rope. And cut the bitter end of the rope off one diameter away from the whipping. Voilà.

Whip braided line in the same way. The only difference is that there are no actual strands to work with, so you have to visualize the strands and sew as if they were there.

Finish detail for a braided whipping.

Of course if your artistic sense rebels against the three cross turns that finish off the whipping being diagonal, you can square them up parallel to the edges of the braided rope (as in the illustration).

If you are making up a piece of rigging of a given length from a long coil or spool of rope, put a whipping on each side of the place where you will cut the rope, leaving a space between the whippings equal to two diameters of the rope. Then cut the rope between the whippings, and your new piece of rigging will be all whipped without danger of unlaying, and the coil or spool will have a whipped end all ready for the next use. That's a satisfying feeling, to achieve two whipped ends with one stroke of the knife.

A special trick having to do with the ends of rope is marrying, which is a way of temporarily joining two ropes, end to end, so that one rope can pull the other through a block. Suppose, on a passage, you discover that a jib halyard has nearly chafed through. You want to replace the halyard without going aloft. Marry the end of the new halyard to the end of the old one, and pull the new one aloft and down through the halyard block with the old one. When the old line brings the new one through the block and your marriage neither parts nor jams, you breathe a sigh of relief and feel grateful you didn't have to go to the masthead.

To marry two ropes, start by putting about twice as much sail twine on your rope needle as you would use for a whipping on one of the ropes. (I assume both ends to be married are already whipped.) Use the twine doubled, as you would for a whipping. On one of the ropes, sew through under one strand at the edge of the whipping farther away from the bitter end. Leave enough end of twine to take two half hitches around its standing part to secure the end of the twine. Place the ropes end to end and sew through under the corresponding strand in the second rope, again at the edge of its whipping farther away from the bitter end. Come back to the first rope and sew through under the next strand, still at the edge of the whipping away from the end. Then go back to the second

---

Marrying two lines. After the second stitch, return to the rope at right and take a stitch under the second of the three strands, followed by a fourth stitch under the corresponding strand of the rope at left. Repeat with the fifth and sixth stitches under the third strands, then go back to the first stitch and retrace the entire circuit for added strength.

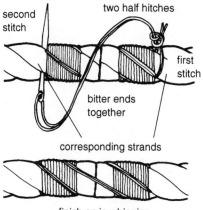

second stitch

two half hitches

first stitch

bitter ends together

corresponding strands

finish as in whipping

rope and do the same thing. Repeat under the third strands of each rope. Now go around again, repeating the process to double up on your "stitches" for extra strength. Pull all these stitches just taut enough to hold the two ropes straight and snug, end to end. Too loose, and a rope's end may hang up in the block; too tight, and the joint will capsize into an angle that won't go through the block. To secure the end of the twine, make your last stitch through the rope and through the opposite strand, as you would make the last stitch of a whipping. Now you have six stitches of doubled sail twine holding the ends of the ropes together, which should be strong enough for the journey aloft and back, yet compact enough to fit through the block. Once the new halyard is all rove off, you just cut the sail twine and take out the stitches. This is one marriage that is planned from the start to be brief.

4 Fittings

When you use rope to make some piece of running rigging, you will be belaying the rope to or reeving it through some fitting. So we'd best now take a tour of a chandlery and get familiar with the fittings you'll need to use.

Fittings, like everything else in boats, have lately been designed and made lighter in weight than they used to be. That's okay, but whenever you buy fittings for a given use, make sure they are big and strong enough to do the job. The installed fittings on many new boats are too small, and nothing is more frustrating than to go to belay a line to its cleat and find that the little thing won't hold enough turns. If a cleat or a block or a fairlead is a bit too big for its rope, that's no problem at all. But if it's too small, then you are in trouble. Replace those small fittings with bigger ones, and if you outfit a boat, make your fittings plenty big to start with. A sailor's traditional bon voyage has long been "Big blocks and small ropes to you!"

Cleats

The function of a cleat is to hold the strain of the line that is to be belayed to it. A proper cleat must be easy to catch a turn around quickly if you need to; take enough turns

23

of the line to hold it securely; provide enough friction for easing a line under heavy strain; and do these things without chafing the line.

There are many designs for cleats. Some have horizontal horns; on others, the horns are slightly raised. The horns may be long or short relative to the base of the cleat. The horns may be circular in section or oval, wider than they are thick. Some cleats have an eye in the base, which can be useful, as we shall see. Cleats may be made of galvanized steel, bronze, or wood. If wood, they must be fashioned of a hard, strong wood, like oak or locust. My preference is for cleats with raised, long, oval horns (smooth, of course), the material of the cleat to go with the type of boat—for instance, galvanized steel for a workboat, bronze for a yacht, and wood for a traditional vessel. A raised horn is easy to catch that first turn around, a long horn will take plenty of turns, and an oval horn will hold the turns best.

Horned cleats.

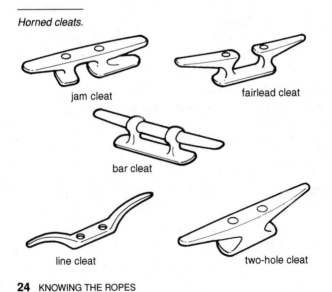

jam cleat

fairlead cleat

bar cleat

line cleat

two-hole cleat

A cleat should be set at a slight angle to the direction of pull of its line. Then the standing part of the line leads away from the cleat and won't jam the turns, so the line may be eased even if it is under heavy strain. But remember that a cleat is designed to be pulled on nearly along its long axis. If you are looking for some place to belay a line temporarily (particularly a line under heavy strain), don't belay in such a way that it will pull across the cleat perpendicular to its long axis, or up on the cleat as if trying to tear its fastenings loose. The line might well succeed!

A totally different type of cleat is the cam cleat. Unlike a cleat with horns to hold the rope, a cam cleat wedges the line between two movable cams. The strain on the line forces the cams against the line, holding it in place. To take in on the line, you simply pull it in. Pulling on the line takes up the strain and so releases the cams. When you stop pulling, the strain forces the cams back against the rope to hold it. To ease the line, you first pull it to release

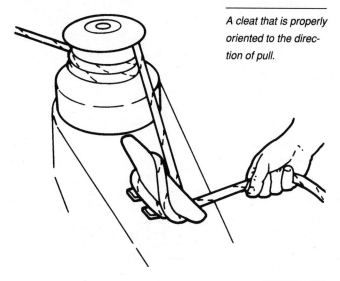

A cleat that is properly oriented to the direction of pull.

the cams, jerk the line up out of the cams, and then ease it. You will have the full strain of the line in your hands, however, which is dangerous if the line is under heavy strain. This is the most important of the cam cleat's three drawbacks. The others are that the line may slip through the cams if the strain gets really heavy, and that the action of the cams may chafe the line. Nevertheless, because a line can be taken in or slacked so much faster on a cam cleat than on a horned cleat, cam cleats are very popular. They are best used on mainsheets, where the tackle reduces the strain to the cleat (and because you adjust the mainsheet often). They should not be used with jibsheets except to secure the tail end of a line wrapped around a winch, in which instance the winch helps take the strain when the line is released from the cleat. They are best used on small craft, where strains are not great.

Through-bolted cleat with backing block.

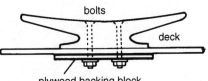

Cleats, wherever possible, should be bolted through the structure that supports them and that structure should usually include a backing block on its inner side. Make your cleats big and strong.

Belaying Pins

Belaying pins serve the same function as cleats but are mounted vertically in a rail. Belaying pins are wonderful things, because if the rail is set up off the deck—waist-height is best—they let you really put your weight into hauling on the line you belay to them. And when you are finished hauling and coil down the line, they make a fine place to hang the coil (about which more later).

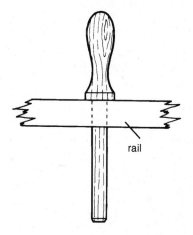

Belaying pins.

rail

Chocks and Fairleads

Chocks and fairleads, like any fitting, should be plenty big and strong. I like Pete Culler's story about how as a young man, he bought himself a pair of big bow chocks he couldn't resist and ended up building his replica of the *Spray* around them.

A chock is a fitting mounted on the rail to hold a line in place so it won't slide along the rail and to protect rail and line from chafing. Chocks may be open or closed. The

Chock configurations.

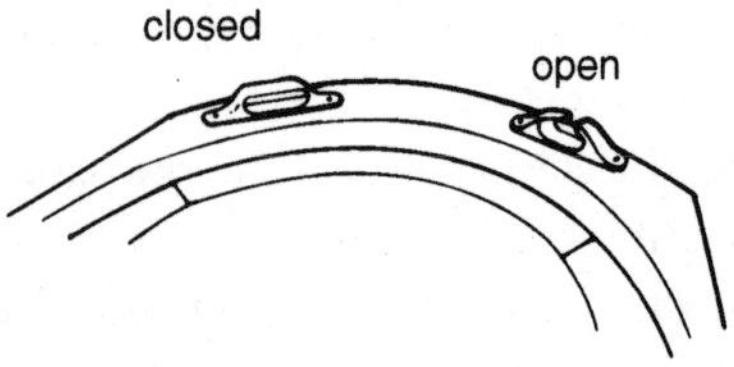

A fairlead block.

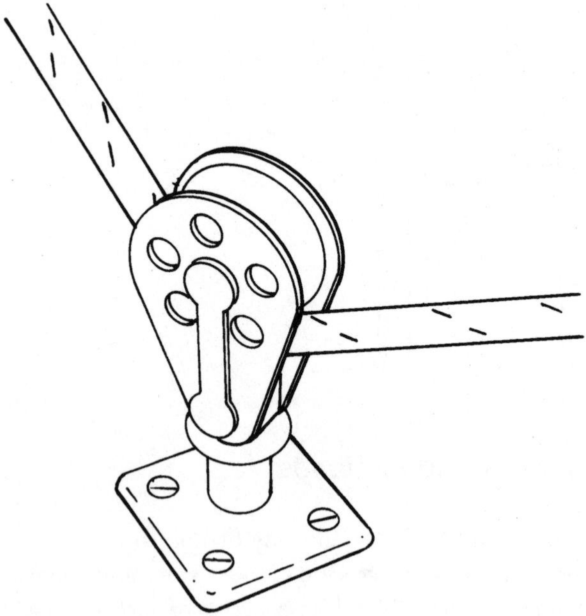

advantage of a closed chock is that the line can't jump out; the drawback is that to get a line into the chock you have to reeve the end through. I prefer the convenience of open chocks. There are also chocks whose tops can be opened by releasing a catch or pin. These are all right, but I always wonder if they are really strong enough to hold in a heavily straining line.

A fairlead may be simply a smooth eye through which a line is led to change its direction of pull so it will lead just right to a cleat or winch. Or, if an eye would produce too much friction, a block may be used as a fairlead, as, typically, on a jibsheet. The rule for chocks and fairleads is big and strong and smooth.

Shackles and Snaphooks

A shackle is a metal fitting used as a link in rigging. It is shaped like a D; the straight part of the D is a removable pin to join the link. The most common forms of shackles are screw-pin; straight pin secured with cotter pin; and snap, which can be opened quickly by pulling out a spring-loaded pin. A snapshackle is convenient if the application requires frequent opening and closing. It is by far the quickest shackle to open and close (keep it well lubricated with oil), and its pin, being always attached to the shackle, can't get lost. I have a great (not always unfounded) fear of losing shackle pins overboard.

The screw-pin shackle is very secure. If you set up the screw-pin with pliers, and especially if you then put a small wire lashing through the eye of the screw-pin and around one side of the shackle, then the shackle will stay securely shut. By contrast, you occasionally hear of a snapshackle popping open when shaken violently or put under extreme strain. The best kind of screw-pin shackle is one on which

Shackles.

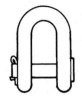

screw-pin shackle   straight-pin shackle

snapshackle

both pinholes are threaded. Then when the shackle is open, the pin is still held by threads and won't be dropped, yet by continuing to unscrew it, you can remove the pin completely if desired.

I see no advantage to a shackle closed by a straight pin and secured by a cotter pin at one or both ends. It is less secure than a screw-pin shackle, and there are more small parts to lose.

I prefer snapshackles on sheet lead blocks, since these blocks tend to get moved around fairly often, and screw-pin shackles on halyards and anchor chains.

A snaphook performs the same function as a shackle, and is quicker to operate, but less strong. Snaphooks have one good use on a boat, at least on a boat that doesn't have roller-furling headsails: They can hold the luff of a headsail to its stay. There are two basic designs of snaphooks, the old-fashioned type with a spring-loaded

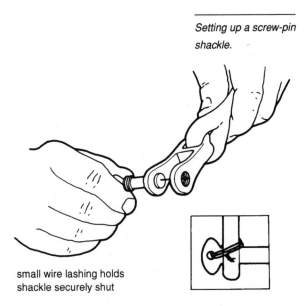

small wire lashing holds
shackle securely shut

"gate" to open or shut the hook, and the more recent design with a spring-loaded piston to perform the same function. I have a strong preference for the gate type, because it can be put on a stay with one hand and usually taken off the stay with one hand. The piston hook, or hank, requires two hands to operate, thus forcing you to

"Gate" snaphooks.

Piston snaphook or jib hank.

violate that basic rule of seamanship, "One hand for yourself and one for the ship"—all too often on a plunging, wet foredeck. Both types of hook require frequent lubrication with oil.

Sometimes you see snaphooks used on boats to fasten lashings that are frequently used at the same length. A sailor may have a lanyard to hold a dodger in the raised position, say, and he gets tired of tying it off every day, so he carefully measures the right length and makes an eye splice through the ring of a snaphook. Now, instead of tying, he can just snap. Ah, but the line stretches a little and then the snapped lanyard is always maddeningly slack instead of being nice and taut. A snaphook used in this way is a snare and a delusion.

Tackles and Winches

To pull "harder than you can" on a rope, you need some sort of mechanical advantage. The common aids are a block and tackle or a winch. You can combine them, leading the fall of a tackle to a winch, and then you have some real power. Before using any kind of mechanical advantage to haul on a rope, look over the whole set-up and see what you may be about to carry away in the process of doing the work you want to do. Is a block lashed to a fitting in such a way that the strain on the line through the block will come on the fitting from a direction that the fitting was never designed to withstand? Are all the fittings involved strong enough to do what you are about to ask them to do?

The way to determine the mechanical advantage of a tackle is to count the number of parts of rope that will be pulling on the work. A main halyard shackled into the

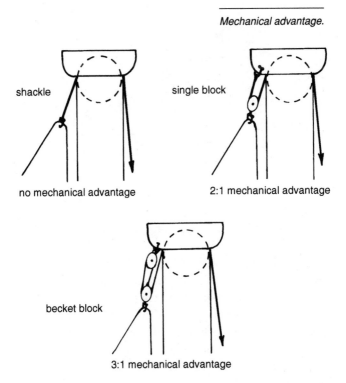

Mechanical advantage.

shackle

no mechanical advantage

single block

2:1 mechanical advantage

becket block

3:1 mechanical advantage

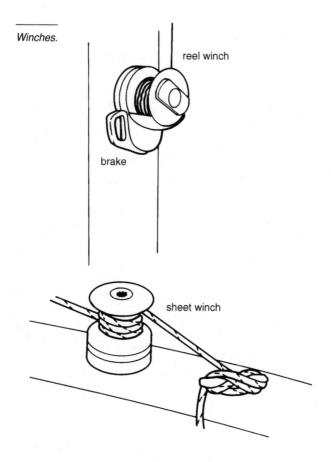

Winches.

reel winch

brake

sheet winch

head of the sail has no mechanical advantage, even though the halyard is led through a block at the masthead. Put a single block on the sail with the halyard led through it, and you have a mechanical advantage of two, because there are now two parts of rope pulling on the sail. Put a single becket block on the sail with the halyard attached to the becket of the block, led aloft through a sheave, back down through the block on the sail, and back aloft through another sheave, and you have a mechanical advantage of three, because there are three parts of rope pulling on the sail. These simple calculations of mechanical advantage discount friction, which will be minimized if you follow the rule of big blocks and small ropes. Use enough blocks to make it easy to hoist your sails and trim your sheets. Make these tasks joyful work, rather than back-breaking chores.

A winch gives you mechanical advantage by the use of a lever arm. The lever is the winch handle, and the amount of mechanical advantage depends on the distance from the edge of the drum of the winch to the part of the winch handle that you grip—obviously, the longer this distance, the greater the mechanical advantage. Again, the admonition is to have winches plenty big and strong enough to do the job.

Removable winch handles are a problem. I'm even more scared of dropping a winch handle overboard than I am of losing a shackle pin. A good kind of pedestal-mounted sheet winch is one with the handle permanently attached at the base of the drum, so as not to interfere with the sheet being wrapped onto the winch. Unfortunately, most winches have handles that you insert at the top of the drum after wrapping the line clockwise around the drum. The best way to stow such handles when they are removed and not in use is in a deep sleeve mounted near the winch.

Wire Halyards

Some sailors prefer wire, rather than rope, for halyards. Obviously, this must be flexible wire that will run over a sheave, not the much stiffer wire used for standing rigging. Some like the halyard to be entirely wire; others prefer a rope tail for the hauling part that will go on the halyard winch. In the former case, a reel winch is necessary to roll up the wire as it is hauled down while hoisting sail. In the latter case, the wire must be spliced to the rope, which is complicated.

The advantages of wire for halyards are that the wire won't stretch as much as rope and that it can be much smaller in diameter than rope for the same strength. The smaller diameter makes for less windage—assuming the halyard is led outside the mast.

Wire or rope-to-wire halyards may have their place in a racing boat, but are, I believe, misplaced in a cruising boat or daysailer. Simplicity and repairability should be the watchwords for cruising gear, and reel winches and rope-to-wire splices are neither simple nor easily repaired. But the great problem with the reel winch is that it must be turned to ease the halyard, so when you go to lower a tightly hoisted sail—or, worse yet, a sailor whom you have hoisted aloft to do some job—you have to hold the winch handle with all your might, release the brake, and pray the thing doesn't get away from you. (Obviously this isn't good enough for the sailor aloft, so we'll discuss later a good way to outwit the reel winch that has been used to hoist a sailor up the mast when he wants to come down again.) In contrast, when you want to ease a rope halyard that's under heavy strain, all you have to do is take it off the cleat and carefully ease the turns around the winch (with the winch handle safely stowed away where it can't whap anybody). With the above considerations in mind, I wouldn't choose wire or rope-to-wire halyards for a cruising boat or daysailer.

Windlasses

A cruising boat of any size ought to have an anchor windlass to break out the recalcitrant hook (or, perish the thought, to kedge the boat off the bottom). The best kind of anchor windlass has a horizontal axle with a drum for rope on one end and a gypsy head or wildcat for chain on the other end. It has a double-action that will turn the axle when the vertically mounted, *long* handle is either pulled aft or shoved forward. If you are upgrading manual systems to power systems, the first consideration should be for a power anchor windlass, especially if you have an all-chain cable.

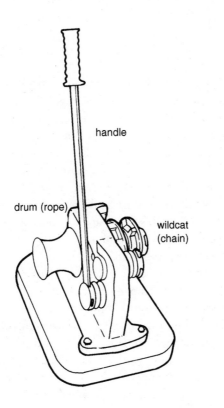

Windlass.

handle

drum (rope)

wildcat
(chain)

5   Handling Rope

A good sailor is always looking around the boat for lines led foul. Has the weather jibsheet gotten under an anchor fluke? Does the jib halyard have a twist around the headstay? Is the spring line to the dock bearing on a lifeline stanchion? Whenever you lead or rig up a line somewhere on a boat, visualize the coming direction of strain and make sure the line leads clear of other lines and obstructions. Whenever you are hauling on a line, whether it be sheet, halyard, dock line, or anchor rode, see that it leads clear before you take a strain on it.

When you are handling any line, watch out for the coming strain on it. Be ready to "catch a turn," that is, take the line around the horn of a cleat away from the direction of strain, or around a post or bitt. Beware of catching a turn round something not designed for belaying, like a lifeline stanchion. If you have a turn around a strong and proper fitting, you can hold a lot of strain on a line. If the strain gets heavy, take another turn or two. With three turns on a cleat, post, or winch, you can hold most any strain you're likely to get on, say, a 40-foot cruising boat, or smaller. On bigger boats, with correspondingly heavier strains, you may need more turns. Towboatmen think nothing of throwing on a dozen turns.

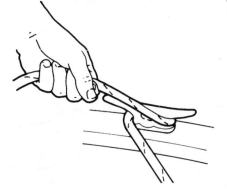

Belaying to a Cleat

Now we come to the important matter of belaying to a cleat. Lead the line to the cleat at a slight angle, if possible (as previously mentioned, the setting of the cleat should allow this), so the standing part can't jam the turns you are about to put on, making it difficult to ease the line later. Take a full turn round the base of the cleat under both horns. Then start your criss-cross turns, putting on as many as you think you'll need to hold the line securely. Then put on another cross-over turn for luck. If the line will be cast off again soon, as with a jibsheet, or if it might need to be cast off quickly, as with a main halyard on a squally night, make your final securing turn go around the cleat again under both horns. Jam the last turn tightly under the last horn. If the line is to be belayed more permanently, as a halyard in settled weather, take a half hitch on one horn of the cleat. You have two choices of direction taking the hitch. Twist it in one direction, and the line rides up uncomfortably over the last turn that crossed the cleat; go in the other direction, and the line lies snugly and securely beside the last turn that crosses the cleat.

Belaying to a cleat. (1) Start figure-eight turns. (2) Final turn goes around cleat, under both horns, ready to be cast off quickly.

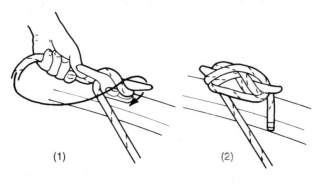

(1)   (2)

When there is no chance that the belay need be cast off quickly, you can dispense with the final full turn and instead tuck the end as shown.

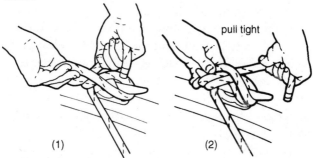

(1)   (2)

Taking a Strain

A way to pull harder than you can on a line (devices to produce mechanical advantage notwithstanding) is to sway, or swig, on it. Say you're in a smallish boat that has no winch for the jib halyard. You haul the jib up taut, but now you want to set it up really hard so you'll have a nice, straight luff in the fresh breeze that's blowing. Take a turn around the halyard's cleat on the mast, grasp the halyard about three feet above the cleat, and, instead of pulling down on it, pull out on it away from the mast, taking care to hold your turn hard as you do so. By pulling out (asking

---

Swaying on a halyard. (1) Pull a bight into the taut halyard with one hand, meanwhile preventing the halyard from slipping around the pin, cleat, or eye with the other hand. (2) Release the bight gradually, taking up the slack you gain around the pin or cleat.

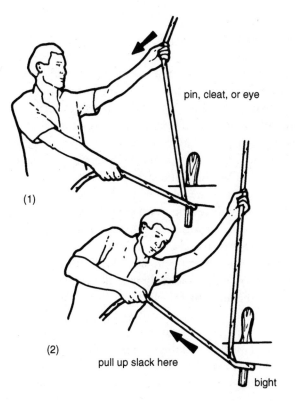

pin, cleat, or eye

(1)

(2)

pull up slack here

bight

the halyard to go extra distance when it wants to go straight), you are exerting a lot of force on the halyard. Now, let the halyard back in against the mast where it wants to go, at the same time taking up around the cleat the slack you've created in the halyard as you let it back. Do this several times, taking up on the halyard a little more each time, and you'll find that you have indeed pulled on the halyard harder than you can.

Swaying works wonderfully well with a team of two. One braces his feet and sways out on the halyard with both hands; the other holds the turn and takes up the slack as the swayer lets the halyard back in to the mast.

Easing a Line

Knowing how to ease a heavily straining line while keeping it completely under control is a worthwhile skill for a sailor to have. First, take a second or two to estimate the amount of strain on a line before you start letting it go. If it has considerable strain, be cautious. Leave three turns on the winch or cleat and work them carefully round as you ease the line that vital first few inches. On lines attached to sails that are full of wind, the first few inches of slack generally reduces the strain considerably. Then you can take off another turn, carefully ease out some more, take off another turn and ease out more. Never allow any slack at all in the line on your side of the winch or cleat; the straining line may suddenly take all that slack in one jump, with the result that the line may fly off the winch or cleat and get away from you (maybe giving you burned fingers or a sprained wrist in the process), or get jammed on the winch or cleat and then be impossible to ease under control. In that case, the only recourse would be to ease, somehow, the strain from the other end (by luffing a jib to ease the strain on a jibsheet, for instance). With the above procedure in mind, you can see the great problem, previously mentioned, when cam cleats are used independently of winches: There's nothing to take turns around to control a heavily straining line as you ease it, a critical safety consideration. Again, on any but small boats, cam cleats should be used for sheets only in conjunction with winches.

Here's a way to take the strain off a line that is jammed on a winch or cleat so you can clear the jam. Secure a strong hauling line to the fouled line about three feet from the fitting on which it's fouled. Use a rolling hitch (coming up on page 64). Heave on this hauling line, using another winch or a tackle if necessary, just enough to take the fouled line's strain off the fitting. With the strain off the jam, you'll be able to clear it. Then replace the line on the winch or cleat properly, and ease off and remove the hauling line.

Coiling

Most cable-laid rope being right-handed, you coil it to the right, or clockwise, or "with the sun" as the old-timer would put it, to help keep it from kinking. When coiling clockwise, twist the rope toward the coil 180 degrees in your coiling fingers as you bring each new loop into the coil. Have the end free, so it can rotate and you can shake and twist the kinks out of it as you finish the coil.

Braided rope may be coiled either way. Braided lines seem to have their own personalities. Some like to be coiled clockwise, some counterclockwise, some one way or the other depending on the day of the week, and some insist on kinking whichever way you coil them. Brion Toss, the rope and knot expert, recommends what he calls

Coiling cable-laid rope.

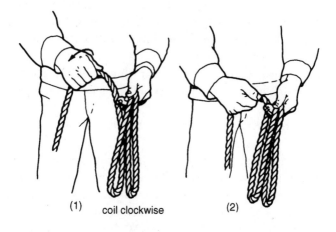

(1)   coil clockwise   (2)

Coiling braided rope. Alternate the normal clockwise coils you use for cable-laid rope with "half-hitch" coils made as in (1) and (2) in this illustration.

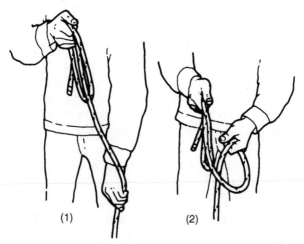

(1)   (2)

"alternate hitch coiling" for braided rope. In *The Rigger's Apprentice* (International Marine, 1985) he writes, "... regular turns that impart twists in one direction are alternated with hitches that impart twists in the other direction. The twists cancel each other out, resulting in a kink-free line." To make the hitches, he says, "... grasp the rope with the back of your hand toward you and turn palm toward you as you bring your hands together."

When coiling a line too heavy to hold in your hands, such as an anchor rode, coil it flat on the deck, making the coil in front of you and taking the line from behind you, between your legs.

If a piece of rope is being naughty and kinking even more than it reasonably should, punish it by throwing it overboard, preferably while underway (making sure one end is secured). Towing the rope for a while will bring it to

Securing a coil to a cleat.

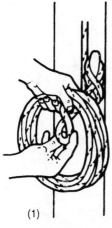

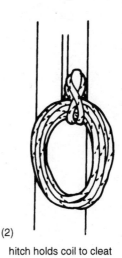

(1)

twist in a hitch

(2)

hitch holds coil to cleat

its senses and let it twist the kinks out of itself. When you bring it back on board, it will be more docile.

A coil of line that is secured to a cleat or belaying pin may be neatly hung on the cleat or pin by taking the part of the line that leads from the finished coil to the cleat or pin, bringing it out through the middle of the coil, and then looping it over the top horn of the cleat or the top of the pin, giving it a twist or two to make it snug.

On some boats you see really fancy ways of making up, or securing, coils of separate lines, such as dock lines. I hate it when somebody hands me one of these works of art as we are sliding in toward the dock and says, "Here, this is the bow line." We're usually all tied up and I'm still trying to find where some hotshot sailor hid the end of my

---

Making up a coil with a square knot.

bow line deep inside an array of neat wraps. Much better just to take the end of a coil, stick it through the coil so the coil is hanging on it between your hands, and then make a quick and simple square knot. Such a tied coil may not

---

Coiling a line for heaving. Check that the coils will run clear and contain sufficient length.

(1)   (2)

win any beauty contests, but it's much quicker to make up and undo again than the fancy-wraps.

A time to be especially careful of coiling is when you're coiling a line you intend to heave to somebody, like a dock line. Coil into your throwing hand more than enough of the line to reach the distance you intend to throw it, taking exceptional care to twist the loops in toward the coil so you won't get kinks. Keep redoing each loop until it's nice and relaxed. Don't throw before you have to (too soon). Aim high, so the line will carry. As with any other throw, bend the knees and follow through with the throwing hand.

To throw a dock line well can be a thing of artistry—and, of course, great practicality. On a little tanker where I performed occasional casual labor, the mate could gather up 25 pounds of bow line and fling it in a great, flat arc so its big bowline would slap right around a piling 50 feet away first try nine out of ten. That acquired skill made some tough landings easy.

Finally, if you need to be sure a line will run out without kinking, a good procedure is simply to work along the

Knot	Security	Tie and Adjust (Under Str
Square knot	Medium	Yes, light strain
Figure-eight	High	No
Bowline	High	No
Two half hitches	Low	Yes, medium strain
Three half hitches	Medium	Yes, medium strain
Round turn & 2 half hitches	Medium	Yes, heavy strain
Round turn & 3 half hitches	High	Yes, heavy strain
Anchor bend	High	No
Clove hitch	Medium	Yes, medium strain
Clove hitch & half hitch	High	Yes, medium strain
Towboat hitch	High	Yes, heavy strain
Rolling hitch	High	Yes, medium strain
Buntline hitch	High	No

line, dumping the bitter end and then the rest of it on deck in as neat a pile as you can. This must be done just before you want the line to run out; otherwise somebody's feet may get into a mutual tangle. Faking a line down like this resists kinking much better than does coiling.

Essential Knots

The accompanying table provides both a preview and a summary of Part Two, A Handbook of Knots. If you need Part Two at all, the table is probably worth a quick preliminary scan, and then, perhaps, a more careful review after you've learned the knots. Although you don't need to know very many knots—this book discusses only nine, with four variations, and recommends you forget two of the variations—you'll find you can't very well use just your one or two favorites for everything. The main reason for needing variety in your knot repertoire is that some of the best knots, like the bowline, can't be tied while the rope is under strain.

Untying (After Strain)	Example of Use
Hard, unless half bow	Tie reef points
Easy	Stopper in end of sheet
Easy	Loop in dock line
Hard	Not recommended; use next knot
Hard	Tie a fender lanyard to a deck fitting
Medium	Tie dinghy painter to post
Medium	Tie dock line to bollard
Medium	Tie anchor rode to anchor
Hard	Not recommended; use next knot
Hard	Tie preventer to boom
Easy	Secure anchor rode to bitt
Medium	Awning tie-down
Medium	Tie dead-end of tackle to becket block

A
Handbook
of Knots

6 The Square Knot and Figure-Eight

The first "real" knot most of us learn to tie is the **square knot**. Its simplicity is intriguing and beautiful, yet it's not really a very useful knot, mostly just good for tying the ends of a line together after you've wrapped it round something, like a package—or a sail. The square knot is good for tying sail stops or reef points (hence its secondary name, the reef knot), but even there it can be improved by a minor modification, which I'll detail shortly.

Some people use a square knot to tie the ends of two separate lines together, for instance, a towline to a dinghy painter, but this should be avoided. If the lines come under heavy strain, the square knot could slip, and, in any case, will jam so as to be hard to untie. Use, instead, two bowlines, as will be explained in Chapter 8.

To tie a square knot, take a turn round one end of the rope with the other end, an overhand knot. Then make a second overhand with the ends and haul taut. You'll have either a square knot or a granny depending on whether you took the second turn the opposite way from the first, to produce a square knot, or the same way, to produce a granny. The granny may slip under heavy strain, is harder to untie than the square knot if it has been under heavy strain, and lacks the nice symmetry of the square knot.

On tying a square knot, most folks start out saying to themselves, "Left over right, then right over left," or vice

Overhand knot.

loose   cinched

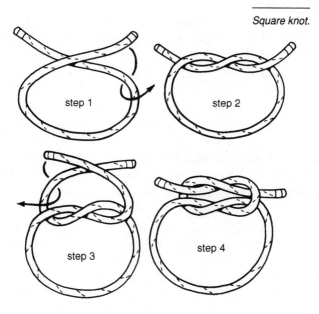

Square knot.

step 1   step 2

step 3   step 4

THE SQUARE KNOT AND FIGURE-EIGHT **53**

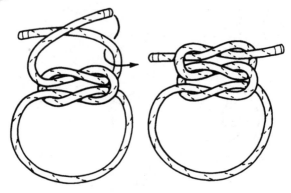

versa, but if you just remember to make the second turn opposite from the first, then it won't matter which way you started.

And pretty soon you'll get so you can visualize the completed knot as you tie it, so if someone handed you the first half of a square knot, you could finish it off without taking the first turn apart to see which way it went.

There is a problem with the security of the square knot and that is that if it is shaken hard enough and long enough, the ends may work loose. If you add a third overhand knot, in the opposite direction to the second one that completed the square knot, you've at least delayed the inevitable; if it shakes loose, you still have the original square knot. Of course, you could go on adding overhands *ad infinitum*, but after about the sixth one, you'd start to wonder if there wasn't a better way. As a matter of fact, though, that's a good way to tie in sail battens: keep piling up overhands, each opposite in direction to the one before, until you run out of line. The leech of a sail will give batten lashings quite a workout every time you tack or luff the sail in a breeze.

You can improve the convenience of the square knot for tying sail stops or reef points simply by forming a bight in one of the ends when you make your second overhand. This creates a sort of half bow. You lose a little bit in security because the knot can't be pulled quite as tight as the bona fide square knot, but for these uses, especially on sail stops, the knot won't be shaken or worried that much. What you gain is handiness in untying the knot: Just a yank on the bow end and the knot comes apart.

If an old whipping comes adrift and you can't take time to replace it right away, a good way to stop the end of the rope from unlaying is by tying a knot in it. A simple overhand knot would accomplish the purpose, but what if it should come under strain? Anyone who has had to work free a tight overhand knot in the end of a line will be cured of tying another. The knot to use is the **figure-eight** knot.

Tie it by making a loop near the end of the line, taking the end round the standing part, and putting the end back through the loop. You have two choices as to which way to put the end through the loop: the "simple" way, in

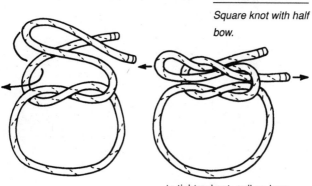

Square knot with half bow.

to tighten knot, pull on loop and opposite end

Figure-eight knot.

one direction, produces an overhand knot; the "complex" way, in the other direction, produces the figure-eight knot.

The great advantage of the figure-eight knot is that it can be untied relatively easily even after it's been jammed tight. To untie a jammed figure-eight knot, work the loop nearer the standing part back over the standing part. This loop of the knot doesn't jam really tight, so it can be worked loose without too much effort; once this part is loose, the whole knot loosens up. We'll see other uses for the figure-eight knot later.

7   Hitches and a Bend

Y ou need hitches to make lines fast to various objects, such as fittings, spars, and the cringles (metal eyes) in sails or awnings, and a bend to tie the anchor rode to the anchor. The great advantage of hitches is that they can be tied while the line is under strain. A mark of a good sailor is the ability to tie a hitch in a straining line without giving up any slack. All hitches start with either a turn or a half hitch around the object being tied to, and the trick is to hold that turn or half hitch firm (to hold the straining line) while you complete the hitch. If you're having trouble holding the straining line, take another turn around the fitting before you tie the hitch.

When tying any hitch, you can either work with the end of the line, or, if you need to tie the hitch in the middle of a long line, you can work with a bight of the line as if it were the end. Be sure to make your bight long enough to tie the hitch comfortably, without running out of bight.

A **half hitch** is as simple a knot as you can form: It's really just an overhand knot. Pass the line through, say, the fitting you want to tie your line to. Cross the end under the standing part and pull it down through the loop formed. Pull the end taut so it parallels the standing part. You have a half hitch. Then repeat by passing the end under the standing part and pulling it down through the loop formed. Tighten, and you have two half hitches—a

57

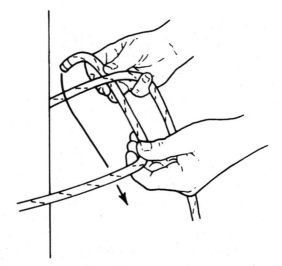

simple but bona fide knot that is reasonably secure. You can also tie your half hitches by crossing over the standing part and putting the end up through the loop formed. The point is that both half hitches must be tied the same way: if you tie the first one by crossing over and coming up through the loop, you must tie the second one the same way, and vice versa.

You can make two half hitches more secure by taking an extra complete turn around or through the fitting before tying the half hitches. The extra turn takes a good deal of the strain, lessening the strain on the hitches themselves. As noted above, it also provides extra friction so you can more easily tie the knot under strain. This is another bona fide knot, the **round turn and two half hitches**. And you can make both these knots more secure by adding a third half hitch.

A specialized knot closely related to the round turn

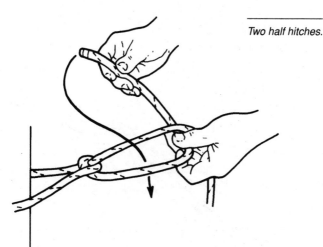

(1)

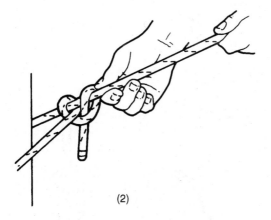

(2)

and two half hitches is the **anchor bend**, used to make fast
the anchor rode to the ring of the anchor. It's simply two
half hitches with an extra turn of the rode around the ring
for extra strength, like the round turn and two half hitches,
except that you tie the first half hitch through the loop
formed by *both* parts around the ring. The usual practice is

Two half hitches, using a bight instead of the end.

Anchor bend.

step 1   step 2

to add a couple more half hitches around the standing part for extra security. If the rode is to stay on the anchor for a while, you might as well seize the end to the standing part with small stuff and be done with it. Then you don't have to worry about the end coming loose.

Another way to look at two half hitches is that it is a **clove hitch** around the standing part. You can also, of course, tie the clove hitch directly around the post. Take the end of the line around the post and bring the end toward you under the standing part. Now take the end around the post again, above the first turn, and bring it toward you, passing the end under the new turn, just over the standing part. Pull on the end and the standing part in opposite directions to tighten the knot.

The clove hitch, if pulled tight, is probably a bit more secure than two half hitches. You can make the clove hitch much more secure simply by adding a half hitch around the standing part after completing the clove hitch. Get in the habit of always adding a half hitch to your clove hitches.

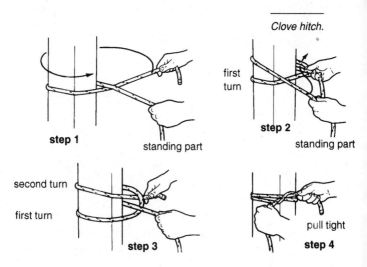

Clove hitch.

first turn

step 1

standing part

step 2

standing part

second turn

first turn

step 3

pull tight

step 4

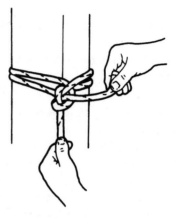

Clove hitch with additional half hitch.

An advantage of both the clove hitch and the round turn and two half hitches is that you can hold and adjust the line under a medium strain with the first turn of the knot and then complete the knot when the line is adjusted to your satisfaction.

If you want to make fast the anchor rode or a dock line to a samson post or bitt, use the **towboat hitch** instead of a clove hitch. Tugboat sailors use it every day, because it is as strong as you want it to be (the more turns you put on, the stronger the hitch), and because there's no way it can jam under heavy strain. If you put a heavy strain on a clove hitch it will jam so tightly that it will be a real job to untie it.

To make a towboat hitch, take the line around the post or bitt, take it under and over the standing part and back around the post in the opposite direction. Give yourself plenty of end (or a plenty long bight, if you're working in the middle of a long line) for more turns. Put on as many turns as you feel are necessary, under and over the standing part and around the post, each turn around the post in the opposite direction from its predecessor. When you have

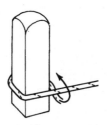

step 1

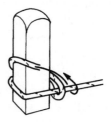

step 2

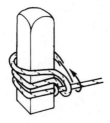

step 3

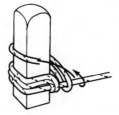

step 4

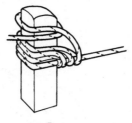

step 5

enough turns, finish off with a half hitch around the post, as if you were finishing off a clove hitch.

The **rolling hitch** is so useful because it will do one thing no other common knot will do: it will grip a piece of standing rigging or running rigging (a taut wire or rope) and won't slip—as long as it's pulled on in only one direction. And, when pulled on in the other direction, the knot can be adjusted. That sounds rather specialized, I know, but no other ordinary knot will do it, so you find yourself tying rolling hitches on the boat every day.

To tie the rolling hitch, begin as if you were tying a clove hitch: Take the end of the line around, let's say, a shroud (instead of a post) and bring the end toward you under the standing part. Take the end around the shroud again, crossing tightly up over the first turn, but again *under* the standing part. Keep these turns tight as you work them. Now finish as in the clove hitch with a turn round the shroud, passing over the standing part and under the new turn. Pull the end toward you and haul taut.

Rolling hitch tied on a shroud.

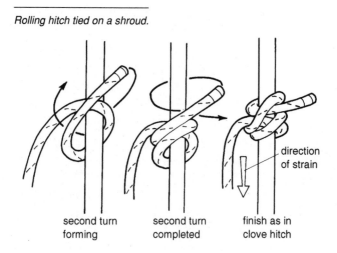

| second turn forming | second turn completed | finish as in clove hitch |

direction of strain

Rolling hitch tied around the standing part.

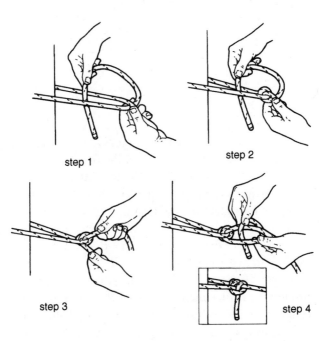

step 1

step 2

step 3

step 4

You'll see that the rolling hitch is a clove hitch with that extra jamming turn in the middle of it. If you now pull down on the standing part, that jamming turn will prevent the knot from sliding down the shroud. (If you pull up on it, however, it will slip.) We'll see a number of additional uses for the rolling hitch later.

Now let's go back to the two half hitches (or clove hitch around the standing part) and tie them with an interesting and extremely useful variation to make the **buntline hitch**. As with other unfamiliar knots, looking at the completed buntline hitch will help you learn to tie it. Look at the drawing of the buntline hitch and you'll see that it is simply

two half hitches (or a clove hitch around the standing part), but that the second half hitch is on the _inside_ of the knot, instead of on the outside, as with two half hitches. This vital difference means that the harder you pull on the buntline hitch, the tighter the end is jammed so it can't slip. It is a very secure knot. An additional advantage is that it can be slid up tight against its fitting. It's the best knot, for instance, to make a line fast to a shackle.

To tie the buntline hitch, reeve the end of the line through the fitting and cross it over the standing part to form a loop, just as if you were starting two half hitches. But instead of pulling the end up through the loop formed, continue it around the standing part _outside_ the loop. Now, continue in the same direction around the standing part inside the loop, and bring the end through to form the second half hitch, or, in other words, to complete the clove hitch around the standing part. Pull the clove hitch taut around the standing part. Slide the hitch up snug against the fitting.

The buntline hitch is one hitch that cannot be tied under strain (otherwise two half hitches would be extinct). It can, however, be untied without much difficulty even when it has been under strain, as long as the strain is not heavy. Just shove the loop nearest the standing part down over the standing part. A buntline hitch that has been under heavy strain can jam.

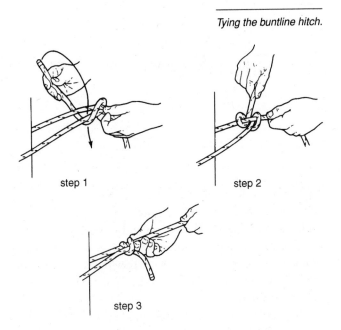

step 1   step 2

step 3

Should you need to make any of these hitches in rope that is especially slippery, add friction by adding turns and half hitches. Then test your new knot before using it. Or, seize the end to the standing part. And test.

8   The Bowline

The bowline is called the King of Knots because it is extremely secure and because no matter how much strain is put on it, it will not jam and can be easily untied. It's used for making a temporary eye, or loop, in the end of a piece of rope. A limitation of the bowline is that you can't tie it in a line that is under strain. Nor is it a knot that can be adjusted once tied.

My father used to tell me I couldn't consider myself a sailor until I had learned to tie a bowline fast with my eyes shut. (But then, of course, after I had learned to do that, it turned out there was a lot of other stuff I had to learn before I could consider myself a sailor.) Anyway, it is true that the ability to tie a bowline without undue hesitation under a variety of conditions is a boon to the sailor.

It will help in learning to tie the bowline if we look first at the completed knot, identify its parts, and see what each part does. Look at the accompanying drawing of the finished knot and you'll see the big loop, formed by the knot, and the standing part, the single line leading away from the knot. If you examine the knot itself closely, you'll see that the end of the line is made into a bight. The standing part leads down through this bight and then takes a half hitch around both parts of the bight. It is that half hitch around the bight that is the secret to the knot's great holding power. The harder you pull on the line, the tighter

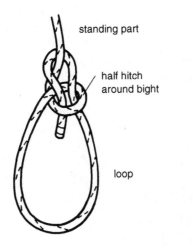

standing part

Bowline.

half hitch
around bight

loop

that half hitch squeezes the two parts of the bight together so the end can't slip free. The top of the bight, running up around the standing part, can remain a bit loose without the knot slipping, because it is the half hitch in the middle of the knot that's doing all the holding. That's the beauty of the bowline: even if it has been under heavy strain, you can still untie it easily by simply working the standing part back down through the top of the bight. A careful study of the way the finished bowline works will help you learn to tie it in a variety of situations.

After some years of struggling to teach the bowline, I have concluded that whoever thought up the story about the rabbit in the hole was a genius. If you follow the story, you can't go wrong: "The rabbit comes up out of his hole, runs round the tree, and goes back down his hole." First, make the "hole" by twisting that small, crucial half hitch into the line where you want the knot to make the desired size loop. Make the half hitch so the end is on top, the standing part underneath. The end of the line is the "rabbit." The standing part is the "tree." Put the end up through the half hitch (the rabbit comes out of his hole), around the standing part in either direction (runs round the tree), and back down through the half hitch (and goes back down his hole). Tighten the knot by grasping the end and the side of the loop that lies alongside it with one hand, and the standing part with the other hand, and pull in opposite directions. Be sure to leave at least six inches at the end to prevent it from slipping back through the hitch.

A quicker way to tie the bowline is to form the half hitch and put the end through it as a single, combined motion at the start of making the knot. Lay the end across on top of the standing part where you want the knot, overlapping by nine inches or so. Wrap the half hitch around the end with the part of the big loop that comes from the standing part. As with alternate hitch coiling (Chapter 5),

Pulling taut.

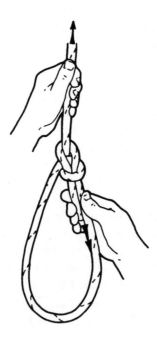

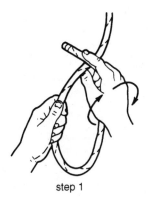

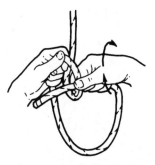

step 1

pivot hand to the right while pinching standing part

step 2

continue pivoting right hand while pulling standing part down to form small loop

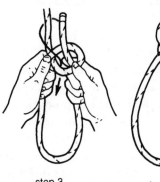

step 3

step 4

when pivot is complete, right hand is palm-to, and end is inside small loop

you grasp the rope with the back of your hand facing you and turn palm toward you as you roll the hitch up and over the end and back toward the standing part. With practice, crossing the end and wrapping the half hitch

THE BOWLINE **71**

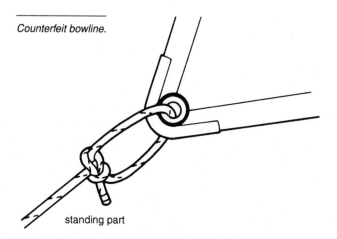

Counterfeit bowline.

standing part

become almost one motion. Complete the knot by bringing the end back around the standing part and through
the half hitch.

Note that the bona fide bowline has that relatively
loose bight around *the standing part*. It is possible to tie
what looks like a bowline with the loose bight around *one
leg of the loop*. But this is a counterfeit bowline, which may
prove valueless. You are most at risk of producing such a
counterfeit when trying to tie the knot around something,
like a mast. Avoid this common error by giving careful
thought to the direction in which you form your hitch. It
must wrap back on the standing part, not down toward
the loop. Using the combined-motion method (rather
than the rabbit method) makes this crucial step easier to
visualize.

Once tying a bowline becomes second nature, you'll
find yourself tying plenty of them every day on the boat.
There are lots of uses for bowlines, as we'll see. A couple of
general uses are to tie the ends of two lines together, and to
form a purchase. To tie the ends of two lines together very
securely, make a bowline in the end of one line, and then

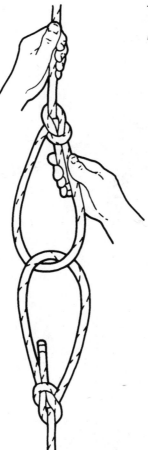

make a bowline in the end of the other line right through
the loop of the first bowline. The two bowlines are like
the links of a chain.

To make a purchase, tie a bowline, with a rather small
loop, in the standing part of the rope on which you want
to pull hard, take the end round something strong and

Tying on jibsheets.

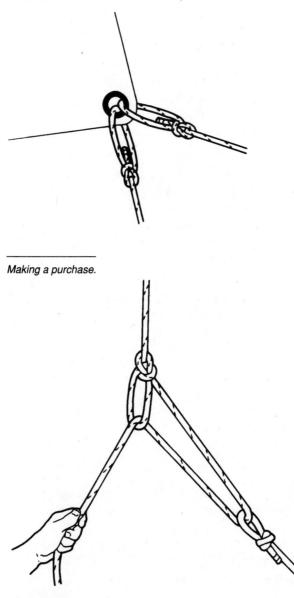

Making a purchase.

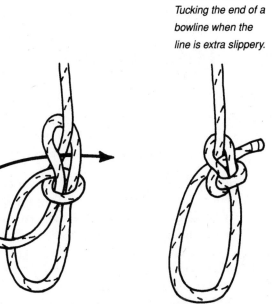

lead it back through the loop of your bowline as if that loop were the sheave of a block. Now pull, and you've got a three-part purchase. It will triple your power, less the friction of the line rendering through the loop of the bowline, which is surprisingly little, especially with braided rope.

We'll see a good deal more of the King of Knots later.

Brion Toss has a neat way of increasing the security of the bowline when tying it in extra-slippery rope: tuck the end of the line back through the loop around the standing part. You weave the end under one side of the loop, over the standing part, and under the other side of the loop.

9   The Eye Splice

Sometimes you'll need a permanent loop or eye in the end of a rope, and then you turn to the eye splice.

We'll deal only with splicing cable-laid rope here; splicing braided rope is a very different technique and you'll seldom need to do it. I must confess I've never needed to make an eye splice in a piece of braided rope. An eye splice is not usually required in the end of a halyard or sheet. If you should use braided rope for dock lines and want loops in the ends of them, it is best to make the loops with bowlines, because you can make the bowline any size you need for a particular docking situation. If you need to make an eye splice in braided rope, look up the technique in Brion Toss's book *The Rigger's Locker* (International Marine, 1992). Brion is a professional rigger; he used 13 pages and 16 drawings to make the splice "human." Better yet, get Brion or another pro to show you how.

To make an eye splice in cable-laid rope, first unlay the rope five untwists. You now have five twists of the three strands separated out. If the rope keeps on unlaying, put a seizing around it at the point where you want it to stop unlaying. And if each strand unlays, put a seizing on the end of each one. These seizings are only temporary, and so may be done quickly with a couple of turns of tape.

Make the size loop you want and lay the end of the rope onto the standing part parallel with it. Make sure the

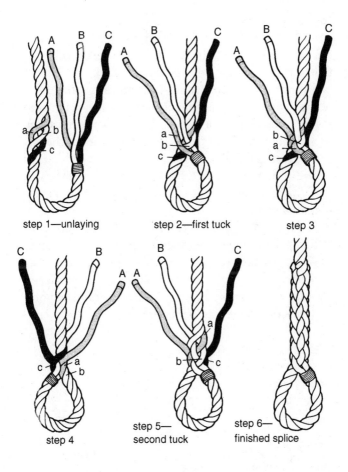

step 1—unlaying

step 2—first tuck

step 3

step 4

step 5—
second tuck

step 6—
finished splice

eye you are making is not twisted and that the unlaid strands lie one on top of the standing part and one on each side of it.

Twist the standing part against the lay to open up a loop under its top strand, and tuck the strand lying on top of the standing part through that loop right to left.

Haul the strand taut along the standing part. Tuck the strand on the left side of the standing part under the strand first to the left of the strand you opened up when you tucked the first strand. Do this by twisting against the lay to open a loop under the strand. Again tuck right to left. Haul taut along the standing part. Tuck the strand on the right side of the standing part under the strand first to the right of the strand you opened up when you tucked the first strand. Open a loop in the same way, and, again, tuck right to left. Haul taut. Now you have made the first complete tuck (of all three strands). Note that each tucked strand comes out between two strands of the standing part. Work the tuck up tight with all three strands hauled taut evenly.

To make the second tuck, take each strand along the standing part, straight ahead, over one strand of the standing part and tuck it under the next strand, opening up the rope by twisting it against the lay as before. Again, haul all three strands taut evenly. Make the third and final tuck exactly the same as the second.

If the rope is tightly laid, a fid will help open up the strands.

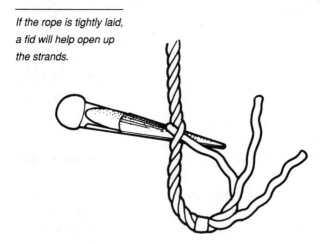

If the rope is so tightly laid that you cannot unlay it enough with your fingers to work the strands through, use a fid to drive through between the strands of the rope to open the loop you need.

To finish off the splice, cut off the strands flush. And to make the splice evenly round and firm, lay it on deck and roll it back and forth under your foot.

Voilà. The eye splice.

If you have to splice extra-slippery rope, use five tucks instead of three for extra security. You can make your eye splice look fancy by tapering it. Add extra tucks and cut out progressively in each tuck more and more fibers from

Eye splice over a thimble.

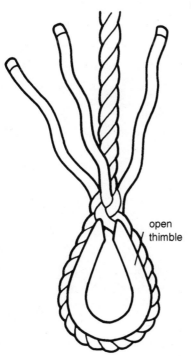

open
thimble

each strand so the extra tucks will each be smaller in diameter as you make them. You can also improve both the appearance and durability of your splice by serving tightly over the splice with marlin.

If the eye in your rope is to be connected to a metal fitting or, say, an anchor, it's good to use a thimble. This is a metal loop shaped like an open or closed teardrop (closed is stronger), concave on the outside of the teardrop and convex on the inside of the teardrop. The splice goes around the outside of the thimble—as tight as you can make it—the rope fitting snugly into the concavity so that the thimble forms a metal liner for the splice. Thus the splice can be shackled to an anchor or, say, the becket of a becket block, without chafing.

THREE

Working with Rope

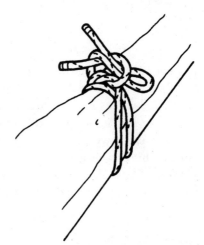

10 Holding Sails to Their Spars

N ow we come to the heart of the matter. We've learned a bit about the make-up of rope, and some essential knots, and we've discussed fittings and gear, mechanical advantage, and some basic techniques of handling rope. Now we can have the fun of going around the boat, putting this knowledge to work by rigging up a number of seamanlike devices that will make sailing the boat and living in her easy and relatively safe.

Bending Sail

Let's start with rigging up the sails. Bending sail doesn't usually require any rope work, because the sails are held to their spars or stays with metal fittings. But fittings can malfunction or break, so it does no harm to know how to use rope to carry out their functions.

We'll begin with bending a sail with a boom. First, secure the tack at the gooseneck. The gooseneck may have a shackle or pin to take the tack cringle. Otherwise, lash the tack cringle to the gooseneck in the position where you want it when the sail is set. Polyester small stuff is good for this lashing. Use as many turns as you can comfortably fit through the cringle. Try to get an even strain on all the turns. Finish off with a triple or quadruple square

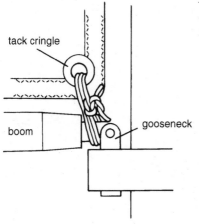

Lashing the tack cringle to the gooseneck.

tack cringle

boom

gooseneck

knot. Or, finish by taking a series of three or four half hitches around all the turns of your lashing, thus binding the turns together and increasing their tension.

Now stretch the foot of the sail aft along the boom. You'll need an outhaul to haul the clew cringle of the sail out, or aft, on the boom to stretch the foot tight. On a small craft, like a dinghy, a good way to rig an outhaul is to tie a line into the clew cringle with a buntline hitch, lead it aft through an eye on the after end of the boom, and back forward to belay on a cleat on the boom far enough forward to be easily reached. With a small sail, you can sway on this outhaul and set it up taut enough without any purchase.

On a sail of 100 square feet or more, you'll want a two-part purchase on the outhaul. Using a buntline hitch, dead-end the outhaul on a becket block on the after end of the boom, lead it forward through the clew cringle, back aft through the becket block, and forward to belay. You have made a tackle using the clew cringle of the sail as one of the "blocks."

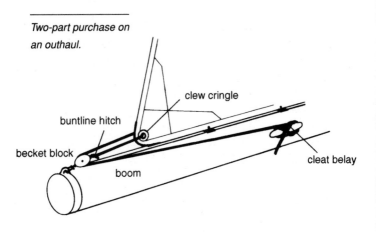

Two-part purchase on an outhaul.

clew cringle

buntline hitch

becket block

cleat belay

boom

On a sail of 300 square feet or more, you'll need more purchase on the outhaul to be able to stretch the foot of the sail as taut as you want it. A good way to get that extra purchase is to rig a tackle on the hauling part of the two-part outhaul described above. Secure the hauling part to a single becket block positioned near the after end of the boom, using a buntline hitch. Dead-end the outhaul tackle to the eye of its cleat (or around its base) forward on the boom with a bowline (make the loop big enough so that the knot will be clear of the cleat), lead it aft through the single block on the hauling part, and back forward to belay. Now you have a two-part tackle pulling on the hauling part of another two-part tackle, which gives you a mechanical advantage of four (you multiply parts when you clap one tackle onto another). With big sails, you can add parts to the outhaul tackle. For example, on a sail of 1,000 square feet, you might want a four-part tackle on the hauling part (double block aft, single becket block forward), giving a mechanical advantage of eight.

The foot of the sail may be attached to its boom with track (on the boom) and slides (on the sail). If so, you slide the slides onto, or into, the track as you haul the clew aft along the boom. Otherwise, the foot of the sail will have grommets every 18 inches or so, and you lace the sail to the boom. Small, braided polyester makes a good laceline. Start at the tack of the sail and tie one end of the laceline into the tack cringle with a buntline hitch. Reeve the other end of the laceline through each succeeding grommet, working aft, and hauling taut each spiraling turn around the boom. Make the end fast through the clew cringle with four half hitches. You may have to go back along the boom again, working each turn up tighter. Make sure the laceline goes around just the boom, not any rigging on it, such as the outhaul.

You can also lace the foot of the sail to the boom by taking a half hitch round the boom with the laceline at each grommet (sometimes known as marling hitches). This method achieves a tighter laceline, but loses an advantage of the spiral laceline, namely that the spiraling spreads the strain evenly among the grommets. I prefer the spiral laceline.

Next, attach the luff of the sail to the mast. If the mast has a track, simply feed the slides on the luff onto it. A good rig is to have a break in the track two or three feet above the gooseneck so you can feed the slides onto the bottom two or three feet of the track, working from tack

Lacing with half hitches around the boom.

"Forth-and-back" method of lacing a small-craft sail to the mast.

luff
mast

to head. Otherwise, you feed the slides onto the bottom of the track, working from the head to the tack, in which case you have to hold up each slide as you feed on the next one.

You can also lace a sail to a mast that has no spreaders, and this method is particularly appropriate to small craft, such as sailing dinghies. Start at the tack and tie the lace-line (say ¼-inch braided polyester, heavier than the small stuff used to lace the foot of a sail to its boom) into the tack cringle with a buntline hitch. Go around the mast and through the lowest grommet in the luff of the sail, then reverse direction and come back round the mast the opposite way, and then go through the next grommet up, and so on. Reverse direction each time you go through a grommet. As you do this, you'll feel as if you're not lacing the sail to the mast at all, but you'll find you are, and this method of lacing will slide up and down the mast more readily than would a spiral lacing. The late, great Pete Culler called it the "forth-and-back" method. I used it to hold the gaff sails to the masts of a tiny schooner I once had, and it worked fine.

To bend a boomless sail that sets on a stay, for instance a jib, start at the tack and secure your tack downhaul to the tack cringle with a strong lashing of small stuff (many turns) or a shackle. Put the snaphooks or piston hanks on the stay, working from tack to head. Attach the sheets to the clew. Attach the halyard to the head. Hoist away.

Furling

Furling a sail in such a way that you end up with a snug roll along its foot is both seamanlike and practical. A well-furled sail can be tightly lashed, which is important because you don't want the sail blowing loose in a gale. After lowering a sail, start the furling operation at its leech, up near the head. Haul the leech aft and dump it into the belly of the sail that you are about to lift. Continue working down the leech in this fashion until you come to the foot of the sail and can roll it up neatly onto its boom and lash it in place with sail stops. When furling a jib that has no boom, you have to hold the foot and roll the sail into it as you near the foot of the sail. Many hands make furling sails light work. If you have to furl a large sail by yourself, get the middle part of the sail under control first and put a stop around it to hold it. Then furl the forward half and tie it in place with stops; finally, work on the after half.

When furling a gaff sail, set the gaff horizontal (using the halyards) and at a height above the boom so that the furled sail will just fit between the two spars. The principle of furling a gaff sail is the same as for Marconi: you work down the leech, haul it aft and dump the sail into its own belly, then roll it up tight when you get to the foot. With a gaff sail, you start this procedure at the peak. Pass the stops around both gaff and boom. Put the first stop back near the after end of the gaff to best control the sail while you finish furling it.

I prefer rope over the usual cloth tape for sail stops just because I like the feel of rope. In any case, have your sail stops long enough to take two full turns round sail and boom with enough end left to make a variety of knots.

A good way to pass a sail stop is to take one turn just around the sail, passing the stop through between the foot of the sail and the boom, and then take the second turn around sail and boom. This method helps hold the sail up on top of the boom. If the foot of the sail is in a groove in the boom, just use two full turns. When putting stops on a headsail with no boom, stretch the sheet taut on the side of the boat where you want the sail, and tie up the sail

Furling a sail. (1) Beginning near the head, haul the leech aft and dump it into the belly of the sail. (2) Continue this process, working down the leech from the head toward the foot of the sail. The belly will steadily diminish as the gathered sail cloth is rolled into a compact bundle. (3) When you reach the foot, roll the bundle up onto its boom and lash it.

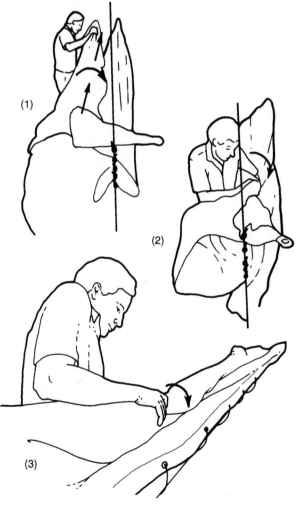

in the straight line in which the taut sheet stretches it, going round with the stops any fittings near the sail, such as a pulpit or a lifeline, to help hold the sail in position.

Once you've passed a stop, haul it really taut, and tie off the ends with a square knot. Or, to make the stop eas-

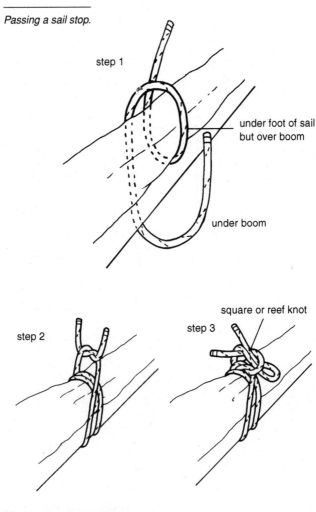

Passing a sail stop.

step 1

under foot of sail but over boom

under boom

step 2

step 3

square or reef knot

ier to untie, use the half-bow knot discussed near the end of Chapter 6. If the sail is big and heavy, a good way to haul the stops taut is to tie a bowline in one end of the stop, pass the other end through it to make a purchase, cinch it up, and then tie it off at the bowline using a half hitch without the end pulled through (so it forms a bight, as in the half-bow knot), and a second half hitch formed with that bight.

Put plenty of stops on your neatly furled sails, and pull them up really taut. Your harbor furl should be able to stand some real breeze without any part of the sail coming adrift. For really heavy weather, in port or at sea, it is a good idea to have a heavy (say, ½-inch) furling line to put on any sail you won't unbend. Start with the line at the head of the sail and put a clove hitch right round sail and boom. Add a half hitch. Now work aft, taking a half hitch with the line round sail and boom every couple of feet. Keep pulling these hitches taut as you go. Finish off at the clew of the sail with another clove hitch around sail and

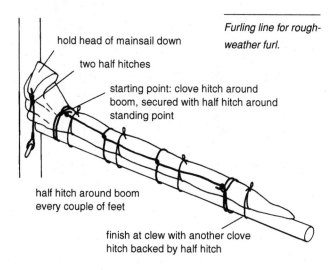

Furling line for rough-weather furl.

hold head of mainsail down

two half hitches

starting point: clove hitch around boom, secured with half hitch around standing point

half hitch around boom every couple of feet

finish at clew with another clove hitch backed by half hitch

boom, again backed by a half hitch. You may need to go back and work each hitch tighter, again working from forward to aft.

Any sail that is usually left bent on should have its own line to hold its head down tight when the sail is furled. A good way to rig such a line is to splice, with an eye splice, the end of a piece of ⅜-inch to ½-inch rope (the same as the halyard size) into the base of the halyard cleat of the sail whose head you want to tie down. Give yourself enough

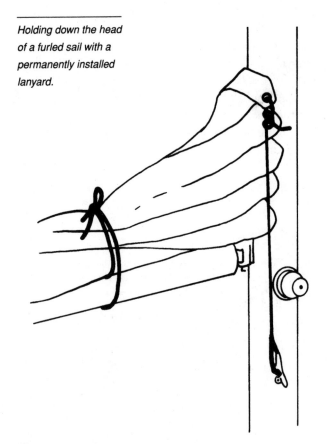

Holding down the head of a furled sail with a permanently installed lanyard.

length to reach up through the head fitting of the sail with enough end to make two half hitches. Put on two whippings and cut her off between them. You now have a handy line, permanently installed, with which you can tie down the head of the sail as soon as you lower it. No more lowered sails climbing partway back up again.

Lashing Down Awnings

Canvas protection over the cockpit is a nice thing to have to keep off wind, rain, or sun. Ingenious yet simple awnings can be designed with panels that can be dropped or lashed up out of the way to meet varying conditions. The best arrangement I ever had was on my skipjack; when it was fully rigged, you were in a huge, totally enclosed screen porch.

All I'm really concerned about here is how you deal with the lashings for your awning. Make them of small braided polyester with some real length, say at least six feet. (Someday you may find a great, new, creative way to set the thing that will require somewhat longer lashings than you first thought. Meanwhile, when you turn those lashings into tackles to haul the awning really taut, the extra length will pay off.) Make the awning lashing fast to the grommet in the awning with a buntline hitch. Lead it through or around whatever you are tying the awning to, go back through the grommet, and haul taut. You have a crude, three-part tackle hauling on the grommet. Tie the lashing off on itself with a rolling hitch, which has the great advantage for this use of being adjustable. You can slide it up or down to adjust the tension on your awning lashings to get them just so. Then, enjoy.

11 Hoisting and Hauling Down Sails

Halyards

Halyards are key pieces of running rigging in any sailing vessel. I've already explained my reasons for preferring rope halyards to wire ones (with or without rope tails), and blocks to reel winches. If you have wire halyards and winches, fine, but you might someday want to switch to rope and blocks. Here, anyway, are some alternate ideas.

Your objectives are to be able to hoist the sail without undue effort, stretch the sail's luff really taut, and lower the sail easily. You need to rig a halyard with enough purchase (mechanical advantage) to be able to hoist the head of the sail up its mast or stay without having to pull with all your might. And you need a way to haul down hard on the tack of the sail to stretch the sail's luff as taut as you want it.

The amount of purchase you need on a halyard depends on the size of the sail. A common error is to have too little purchase. Making sail should be a joyful thing—after all, it immediately precedes the excitement of getting underway—but hoisting a sail that is too hard to pull up can take the joy out of it.

Tiny dinghy sails need no purchase at all. Just tie the halyard into the cringle in the head of the sail with a bunt-line hitch, lead it up through a single block aloft or sheave in the masthead, and down to a cleat on the mast. (A good

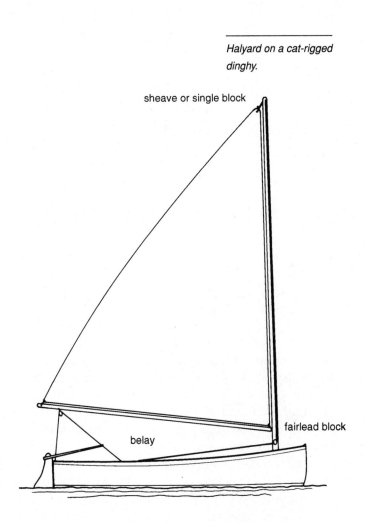

sheave or single block

fairlead block

belay

trick in a very small, cat-rigged dinghy, in which you'd rather not put your weight right up in the bow to reach the halyard cleat, is to lead the halyard through a block at the foot of the mast and then aft to belay to a cleat on the inside of the gunwale, or on the centerboard trunk. Then you can hoist or lower the sail with your weight in the middle of the boat.)

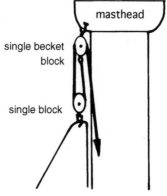

Halyard with two-part purchase.

As soon as a sail gets up to any size at all, say 100 square feet, it needs a halyard with a two-part purchase. Using the buntline hitch, dead-end the halyard on the becket of a single block aloft (positioned a foot above the point where the head of the sail will be when it is set), lead it down through a single block shackled into the cringle in the head of the sail, or into its headboard, back aloft through the becket block, and back down the mast to belay. This rig lets you hoist the sail aloft with the greatest of ease and will work well with a sail of some real size, say up to 750 square feet. The two-part purchase makes all the difference in the world.

It's always a good idea to secure the hauling end of a halyard so it can't go aloft by mistake. If you make a habit of keeping the halyard end tied through the eye of its cleat with a bowline (with a loop big enough to keep the knot of the bowline well away from the cleat so that the knot won't interfere with belaying to the cleat), then you will never have to go aloft after a lost halyard.

Downhauls

To haul the tack down so as to stretch the luff taut, you need even greater purchase, so you can set that luff up really hard (as for a strong breeze). Even a tiny dinghy sail will profit from a two-part purchase on the tack downhaul. (Set your luffs taut with downhauls, not halyards; don't fight gravity, use it.) Dead-end the downhaul on its cleat at the foot of the mast. If the cleat is wood, you can drill a hole sideways through its base, just big enough to take the line for the downhaul. Reeve the downhaul through the hole, and tie a figure-eight knot in the end to secure it. If the cleat has an eye, you can splice the dead-end of the downhaul into it with an eye splice. Then lead the downhaul through a single block at the tack of the sail. On a boomed sail, the block would be secured to the underside of the boom at the gooseneck or jaws. (The boom, of course, must be free to slide on the mast on a track, or with jaws.) Then lead the downhaul back down to belay on its cleat at the foot of the mast. (To get the downhaul amidships in a small dinghy so you don't have to go forward to handle it, dead-end the downhaul to a heavy screw-eye at the foot of the mast with a buntline hitch, lead it up through its block, back down through a lead block shackled to the screw-eye, and aft to its cleat on the gunwale or centerboard trunk.)

At 100 square feet or more, a sail needs a three-part purchase for the tack downhaul. Dead-end the downhaul on the becket of a becket block on the boom, lead it down through a single block at the foot of the mast, back up through the becket block, and down to its cleat. At 300 square feet, a four-part purchase is none too much for the tack downhaul. Dead-end on a becket block at the foot of the mast, go up through one sheave of a double block on

Three-part purchase on a tack downhaul.

single becket

single block

the boom, down through the becket block, up through the second sheave of the double block, and down to belay. These tack downhauls are short tackles, and you want to be able to sway them down hard.

For a headsail set on a stay, all of the above is applicable. The upper block of the downhaul tackle is shackled into the tack cringle of the sail, and the lower block is shackled to a strong fitting just abaft the lower end of the stay. The lower block will, in each case, need an extra sheave at the foot of the stay to lead the downhaul aft to belay to a cleat on deck. This cleat can be back near the mast, so you don't have to go way forward to sway the downhaul. (And the taut, strong line along the foredeck will not be amiss when she's pitching into it, well heeled over, and you're looking for something extra to hang onto as you crawl to the bow to check your anchor lashings, or whatever.)

You don't often see the rigs described above. What you usually see on a sail of, say, 300 square feet is a halyard

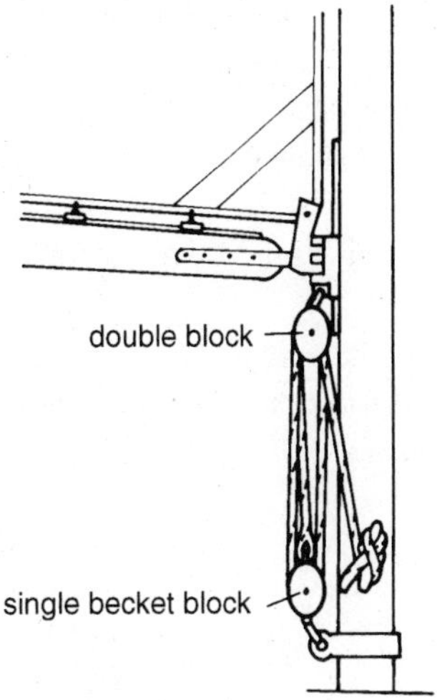

Four-part purchase on a tack downhaul.

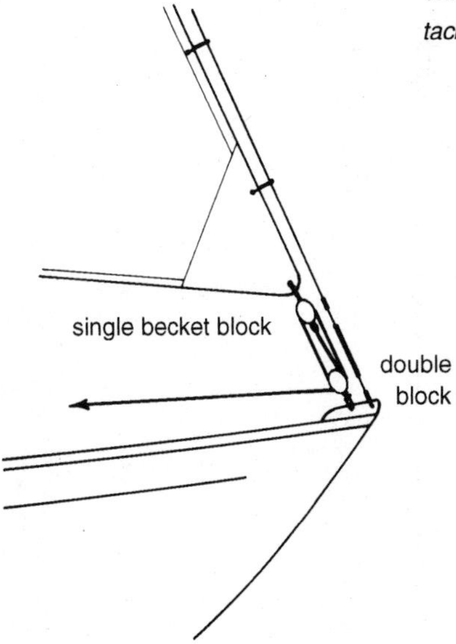

double block

single becket block

Three-part downhaul tackle for a headsail.

single becket block

double block

with no purchase, a winch, and, as often as not, a fixed tack. Let's look at the advantages and disadvantages. My double-purchase halyard has to be twice as long, has twice as much windage and weight aloft, and has an extra block, plus the tack downhaul paraphernalia. In theory, it takes me twice as long to hoist my sail. In practice, my sail goes

---

Halyard rigs compared. On the left is a common production sailboat solution. On the right is my preference.

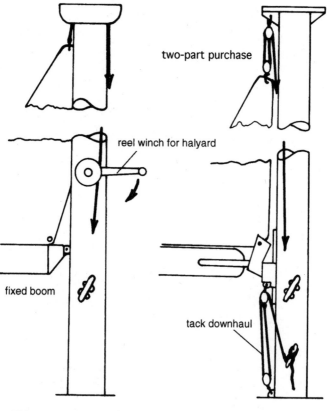

two-part purchase

reel winch for halyard

fixed boom

tack downhaul

up nearly as fast with much less effort, because I can just hoist steadily, hand over hand, while the no-purchase hoister would be shifting his position, getting a better grip, and wondering if something's not stuck aloft. And I haul down the tack more quickly and easily than one could winch up a sail to set the luff up taut. I spare the expense of the winch. I never have to look for the winch handle, nor will I ever lose it. I'll never be handicapped by a malfunctioning winch. My sail is a bit harder to pull down in a strong breeze because of having to "overhaul" the two-part tackle as it comes down. I think the trade-offs are worthwhile in the direction of a two-part halyard and a tack downhaul with real power.

Sometimes you need to get the sail you hoisted back down again in a hurry, as in a sudden squall. The piece of rigging that will enable you to do this is the downhaul—not the tack downhaul, but a separate downhaul rigged

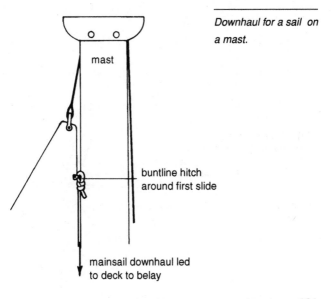

Downhaul for a sail on a mast.

mast

buntline hitch
around first slide

mainsail downhaul led
to deck to belay

to the head of the sail, by which the sail can be bodily hauled down the mast or stay even though the wind is putting a hard strain on the luff fittings.

A good way to rig such a downhaul for a sail on a mast is to tie the bitter end of the halyard around the first luff fitting (sail slide or mast hoop) below the head of the sail, using a buntline hitch. Don't tie it into the very head of the sail, because then the downhaul would put a twisting strain on the topmost luff fitting, which might cause it to jam. When you hoist the sail, the end of the halyard goes aloft with it and gives you a way of hauling the sail right down the mast with all your weight, if necessary. One time while sailing my skipjack, I got surprised by the wind sud-

---

Downhaul for a headsail on a stay. It should be long enough to belay with the sail hoisted.

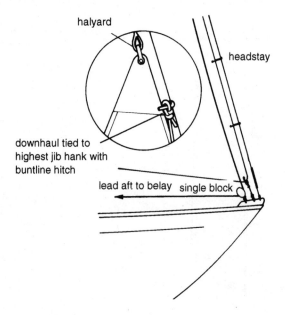

halyard

headstay

downhaul tied to
highest jib hank with
buntline hitch

lead aft to belay   single block

denly breezing on hard and was able to haul down her 600-square-foot mainsail very quickly, possibly saving the mast or even a sinking, because all I had to do was let go the halyard and haul down hard on its end, which was tied into the topmost masthoop on the sail.

For a headsail on a stay, it is best to rig a separate down-haul because the downhaul has to pull down along the stay, not down the mast, which is where the end of the hal-yard would lead if sent aloft with the sail. Tie the down-haul (it need not be as strong as the halyard) into or around the topmost snaphook (not the head of the sail, for the same reason as previously mentioned) with a buntline hitch. Lead it through a lead block at the foot of the stay and aft to belay near the sail's halyard. To take in the sail quickly, let go the halyard and haul on the downhaul. Down she comes—and down she stays when you make the downhaul fast. You didn't even have to go forward to the stay, an advantage that will be particularly appreciated if the stay leads to the end of a plunging bowsprit.

Showing Your Colors

It's nice to have a flag halyard to hoist a pennant to the masthead or a flag to a spreader. Make your flag halyards out of small, braided polyester. All you need is a small, sin-gle block at the point on mast or spreader where you want the flag to fly with the halyard led through it. On a mast-head flag halyard, tie the ends together with a square knot, pulled up hard, to make the halyard into a continuous line, so one end can't accidentally go aloft. The pennant will need to be attached to a pigstick, a dowel say, of ⅝-inch diameter and about three feet long, so the pennant will fly above the masthead in the clear. Cut a vee-shaped groove around the circumference of the pigstick at the

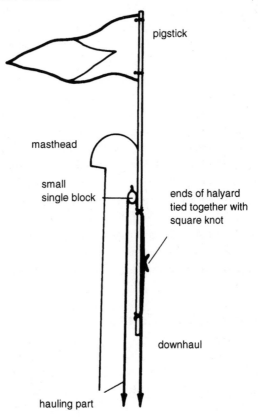

Flag halyard. Pull the flag up with the hauling part, then tighten the downhaul part to bring the pigstick vertical. Belay the two halyard parts together on deck.

pigstick

masthead

small
single block

ends of halyard
tied together with
square knot

downhaul

hauling part

points where each grommet on the pennant will come, and lash the grommets to the pigstick with sail twine, fitted into the grooves. To make fast the pigstick to the halyard, take the halyard just above the square knot and make a clove hitch around the pigstick at its midpoint, then stretch the halyard down to the foot of the pigstick and make another clove hitch around the pigstick a couple of inches from its lower end. The part of the halyard stretched taut along the pigstick between the clove hitches should contain the square knot. Hoist away, keeping a little tension on the slack part of the halyard leading down from the lower end of the pigstick.

On a flag halyard to a spreader, you won't need a pigstick, because the flag merely flies beneath the spreader. Tie the ends of the halyard together with a square knot so the halyard can't accidentally unreeve through the block on the spreader, but don't pull the knot up really hard, because you'll be untying it each time you bend on a flag to hoist. Simply tie one end of the halyard into the upper grommet of the flag with a buntline hitch and the other end of the halyard into the lower grommet with the same knot. Hoist away.

Hoist your pennant or flag right up as high as it will go and then take a good tension on the lower part of the halyard so the flag will stand vertically. Nothing is worse than seeing a pigstick at a 45-degree angle, or a flag with a droopy luff (all U.S. Post Office personnel please take note). If you don't have a cleat on which to belay your flag halyard, you can make it fast around a turnbuckle with a rolling hitch or through a turnbuckle with half hitches.

12 Trimming Sails

One of the nicest jobs a sailor does is to trim the sails. It's so satisfying to make minor adjustments to the angle a sail is making with the wind, get it trimmed as perfectly as you can, and watch the boat respond with a bit more speed.

The piece of rigging you use to trim a sail is, of course, its sheet. The same old rules are absolutely fundamental to sheets. Make your sheets strong enough—and big enough to be easy to hold onto. Give them plenty of purchase, and use blocks big enough to reduce friction. On a day when the wind is flukey, you'll be trimming sheets dozens and dozens of times; each time you trim a sheet should be a pleasant task, not a grating chore. Following the above basic rules will make it so.

Boomed Sails

Let's talk first about sheet rigs for sails with booms. Any sheet, even on a tiny dinghy, should have at least a two-part purchase. In a small craft that can tip over in a gust if her sheet isn't eased smartly, you tend to hold the sheet in your hand, certainly whenever you are sailing to windward in a breeze, and plenty of other times, too. Some prudent sailors make it a rule never to belay the sheet in a small craft. Anyway, the point is to make the sheet big enough to be comfortable to grasp for a long time. This means it should be at least ⅜-inch rope and preferably ½-inch, even though such sizes give far more strength than is necessary.

For a two-part sheet in a small craft, like a sailing dinghy, dead-end the sheet to a shackle or snaphook on a traveler, with a buntline hitch, lead it through a single block well aft on the boom, then through a lead block on the boom, positioned so the sheet will fall vertically from the lead block to your sail-trimming (non-steering) hand when you are seated comfortably at the tiller.

The purpose of the traveler is to be able to trim the sail to the lee quarter, rather than amidships, to take some

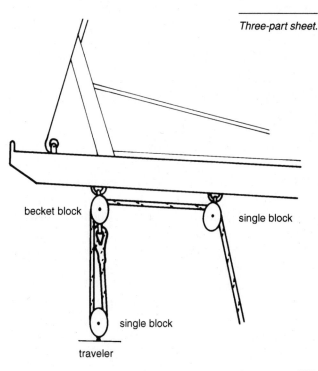

Three-part sheet.

becket block

single block

single block

traveler

of the twist out of the sail. A good traveler in a small craft can be made of a stout piece of rope reeved through an eye on each quarter of the boat, and secured with figure-eight knots on the outboard sides of the eyes. The rope should have enough slack to lift well clear of the tiller. Bigger boats will have metal rod or track travelers. Generally the length of a traveler should be something like half the beam of the boat.

Once a sail reaches a size of 75 square feet or more, you need a three-part sheet. Remember, use plenty of purchase; make your sheet a joy to trim. Use big blocks so the sheet will slack easily too. To rig a three-part sheet, dead-end on a becket block well aft on the boom (buntline hitch, naturally or even an eye splice on a thimble if you want to get fancy), then down through a single block on the traveler, led from forward to aft, up through the becket block, led from aft to forward, and forward along the boom to the lead block to bring the sheet down to a convenient belaying point. Or, if the most convenient belaying point is aft, down to a lead block on deck and to its cleat.

For a sail of 200 square feet or more, rig a four-part sheet. A good way to rig a four-part sheet eliminates the traveler. Dead-end to an eye-bolt through the deck abreast the after part of the boom and off the centerline at about where one end of a traveler would be. Lead up through a single block well aft on the boom, from aft to forward, down through a single block on deck, positioned where the other end of the traveler would be, from forward to aft, back up through a second single block, also well aft on the boom, from aft to forward, and to the lead block, either on deck or on the boom, leading to the belaying point. With this rig, the boom can be hauled down hard to leeward to take some twist out of the sail when trimmed close-hauled, giving the same effect as a traveler.

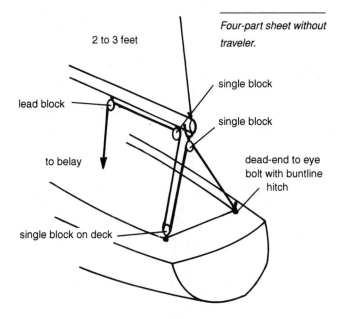

Four-part sheet without traveler.

single block

lead block

single block

to belay

dead-end to eye bolt with buntline hitch

single block on deck

A nice modification to the above-described four-part sheet is to rig it double-ended, so there will be two hauling parts, one on each side of the boat. With this rig, when the boat is well heeled over, you can always work the main-sheet on the windward side. Rig the double-ended, four-part sheet as follows: Start at the belaying cleat on the star-board side, say; go through a starboard, single deck block, positioned, as above, where the end of a traveler would be, from forward to aft; go up through one sheave of a double block well aft on the boom, from aft to forward; down through a single deck block on the centerline, from forward to aft; up through the second sheave of the double block on the boom, from aft to forward; and down through a port, single deck block, positioned where the port end of the traveler would be, from aft to forward; then to the port belaying cleat. Now, that's a beautiful piece of block and tackle work, always a joy to use.

Double-ended four-part sheet. Here the deck blocks ride on a traveler car, and self-tailing winches finish off the rig. Sometimes the "low-tech" solution is more appropriate: Eliminate the traveler and winches, move the two off-center deck blocks outboard port and starboard to or beyond where the traveler ends might have been, and lead the sheet ends through these blocks to belay on cleats.

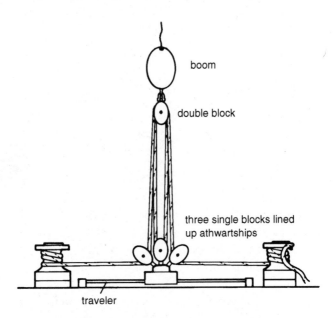

boom

double block

three single blocks lined up athwartships

traveler

These four-part sheets are good for a sail with an area of, say, up to 500 square feet. With bigger sails than that, add more parts to your sheet, up to six. Six parts is about as much tackle as you can conveniently ease off when slacking the sheet, without making a big job of overhauling it. If your sail is so big that a six-fold purchase is hard to haul in in a breeze, then you need to add a winch.

Sails Without Booms

Now, let's talk about sheets for sails without booms, like headsails. Many sailors tie a sheet into the clew cringle of a jib with a bowline. I have a slight preference for the bunt-line hitch, because it lies more snugly to the sail and seems to hang up less on the shrouds. I know the modern way is to rig jibsheets as single parts with no purchase and use winches to haul in these heavily straining sheets. But I'd like to make an argument for the two-part jibsheet. On a sail of 100 square feet or more, you'll still need a winch to trim a two-part sheet, so elimination of the winch can't be part of my reasoning, except for sails of less than 100 square feet. I just like the idea of halving the strain on the sheet you are winching in. This leads to fewer mashed fingers, fewer jammed turns on the winch, finer adjustment, and fewer incidents of the sheet's getting away from you when you go to slack it. Yes, you do have more sheet to winch in, but still not a lot with only two parts.

If your jib has a nice big clew cringle, it's a simple procedure to rig a two-part sheet. Using a buntline hitch, dead-end the sheet to an eye-bolt on the lee deck, forward (one sheet on each side of the boat, of course), lead it through the clew cringle from inboard to outboard, then aft through a lead block on the lee deck, amidships, and back to the winch. The friction on the cringle is surprisingly little more than that of a block.

The positioning of the dead-end of the sheet and of its lead block needs careful working out. These fittings are often on tracks to give flexibility and to allow them to be used for different sizes and shapes of jibs. Suffice it to say that the object of positioning these fittings is to end up with a sheet that hauls on the clew of the jib about perpendicular to its stay, or, to be more precise, in such a direction that when the sail is trimmed flat for sailing close-hauled, the foot and leech will be stretched about evenly taut, but on no account with the leech more taut than the foot.

It's a good idea to tie a figure-eight knot in the end of any sheet, so that if it gets away from you, it can't unreeve.

13 Holding Booms Steady

The Topping Lift

A most useful piece of rigging in any boat with a boom is the topping lift, a line rigged to hold the boom up when the sail is down. I can't fathom why, but some sailors struggle to sail their boats, particularly small boats, without the benefit of a topping lift. So they have to remember that when they drop the sail, down will come its boom, too, sometimes with a bang, sometimes to peril of life and limb. Rig a topping lift. It's worth it. It's just like having an extra crewmember on board who will slavishly, uncomplainingly, take care of the boom at all times on his own initiative. The boat I'm sailing as I write this, the aforementioned well-rigged ketch, unaccountably had no topping lift on the main boom. One of my first jobs on board was to rig one.

Here's a good way to rig a topping lift. Use a strong line, as strong as the halyard. Dead-end the lift at the after end of the boom with a buntline hitch to an eye-bolt, lead it aloft to the masthead through a single block positioned above the halyard block if possible, but in any case as high as is practical, and down the mast to belay. In a small boat, with a light boom, that's all you need. (In a tiny dinghy, again, lead the topping lift aft through a lead block so you can work it with your weight amidships.) On a sail with an

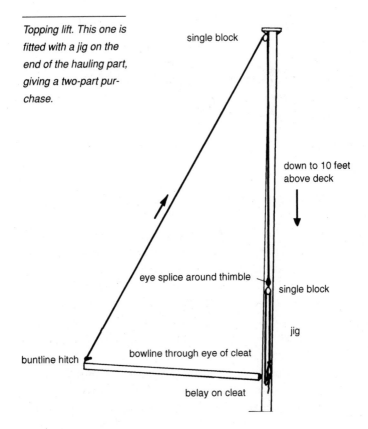

Topping lift. This one is fitted with a jig on the end of the hauling part, giving a two-part purchase.

single block

down to 10 feet above deck

eye splice around thimble

single block

jig

buntline hitch

bowline through eye of cleat

belay on cleat

area of 100 square feet or more, the boom will be heavy enough so that you will need some purchase on its lift. (When rigging a topping lift, visualize a couple of heavy sailors reefing the sail with the boat rolling heavily, their beefy bodies lurching to leeward against the boom; these sailors [you?] may occasionally have to depend on the lift you are rigging to be able to take such heavy, sudden strains.)

A good way to add purchase to a topping lift rigged as described above is to put a jig on the hauling part. A jig is a tackle on the hauling part of a piece of rigging enabling you to haul on that piece of rigging harder than you can. End the hauling part of the lift 10 feet above the deck with an eye splice with a thimble in it. Shackle a single block into this thimble. Dead-end your jig at the cleat for the topping lift on the mast (with a bowline through the eye of the cleat, its loop big enough so the knot won't interfere with belaying), lead it up through the single block on the hauling part of the lift, and back down to belay. That gives you a two-part purchase. Be generous with the amount of purchase on your topping lift. For a sail area of 200 square feet, use a three-part jig, with the upper block a becket block, and the lower block a single; for 400 square feet, use four parts, with the upper block a double block, and the lower block a becket block. Later, we'll discuss handy ways to use a boom that can be raised ten feet with a powerful tackle.

Again, you don't often see topping lifts rigged as described above. Often they are of wire for strength with less windage. But windage is not very important at the trailing edge of a sail, and wire chafes the leech of the sail more than rope will. And instead of the lift being led aloft and down the mast, it often dead-ends aloft and has a short tackle for purchase on the boom. But the boom may be swinging wildly when you need to work its topping lift, so the tackle to work it will be swinging wildly too, maybe high over the cockpit or out over the water. It's much better to be able to go forward and work the lift at the mast.

Lazyjacks

If having a topping lift is as good as having an extra hand on board, having a set of lazyjacks is as good as shipping two or three sailors you don't have to feed. Lazyjacks keep a boomed sail up on the boom when the sail is lowered, instead of letting it fall all over the deck, in the water, or in the helmsman's eyes. For a sail of any size, you'd have to ship more than one extra sailor to perform such duty. So, if your boom is, say, 12 feet long or more, lazyjacks make sense.

A good way to set up lazyjacks is to rig two, one on each side of the boom. They need not be as strong as the halyard or topping lift. Small, cable-laid polyester is a good choice. Dead-end each lazyjack to an eye fitting about two-thirds of the way up the side of the mast; using a buntline hitch, lead each through an eye fitting on its own side of the boom about two-thirds of the boom's length abaft the gooseneck; and make each fast back on itself with a rolling hitch, leaving about three feet of end so you'll have plenty for adjustment. This gives you a point two-thirds of the way aft along the boom at which the lowered sail will be held up on the boom. Now, to get another such point one-third of the way aft along the boom, use a rolling hitch to tie a second leg to each lazyjack about halfway up its length. Lead each new leg to an eye fitting on its own side of the boom a third of the way aft on the boom, and make fast with a rolling hitch, again leaving a three-foot end. Now you have the equivalent of two sailors stationed strategically along your boom ready to catch your sail when you lower it and hold it until you are ready to furl it. On big boats with long booms, more legs can be added to the lazyjacks as necessary.

The drawback to lazyjacks is that there can't be much wind in the sail when you hoist it, or the sail will blow off to leeward and bear against the lee lazyjack, possibly getting hung up in the process. That's the time to slide your rolling hitches all the way down to their boom fittings on the lee side to give the lee lazyjack as much slack

Lazyjacks.

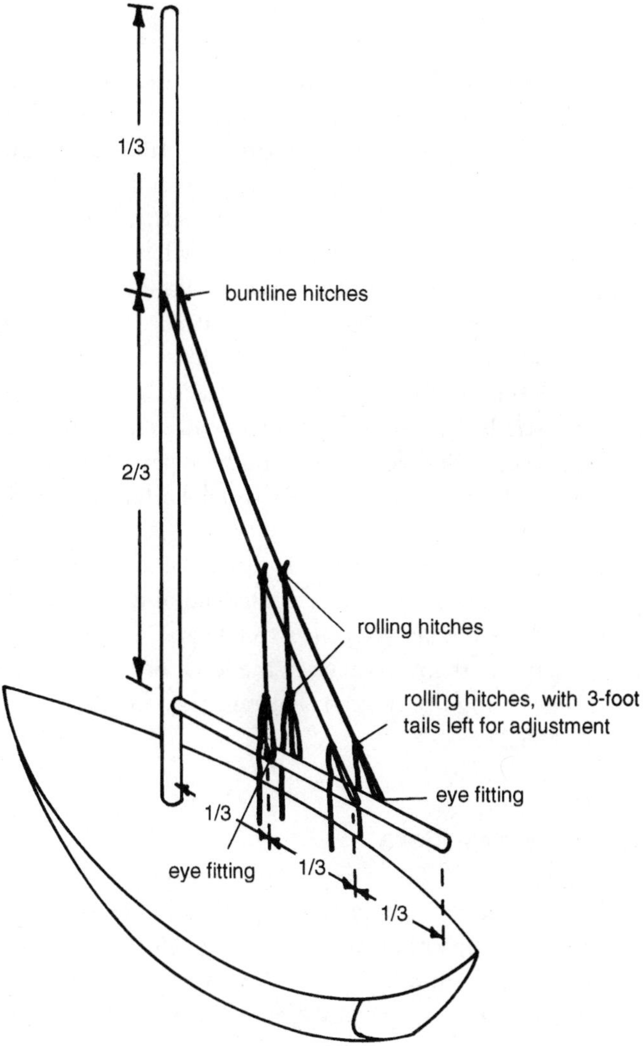

1/3

buntline hitches

2/3

rolling hitches

rolling hitches, with 3-foot
tails left for adjustment

eye fitting

1/3

eye fitting   1/3

1/3

as possible. And slack the sheet and/or head the boat up closer to the wind to relieve the pressure on the lee lazyjack.

Battens are the nemesis of lazyjacks, because they tend to get hung up on them. Ideally, if you're in a position to buy new sails, lazyjacks and a battenless sail make a good combination for cruising. A battenless sail must have a slightly concave leech (so it won't flutter), whereas a sail with battens gains a little extra area by having a slightly convex leech. The loss of area is a valid trade-off, I think, for the simplicity of not having battens. At the other extreme, fully battened sails, in which the battens extend from leech to luff, work well with lazyjacks while saving that extra leech area and enhancing sail shape. These too deserve consideration. But if you have partial battens in your sail, lazyjacks are still worthwhile despite the hangups.

A gaff rig works fine with lazyjacks, because you rig the after legs to be forward of the after end of the gaff, so the gaff always lies between the two lazyjacks and goes right up between them. Battens in the leech of a gaff sail can still get hung up, though. For more on the gaff rig, see Chapter 15.

Jibe Preventers

While sheets are to hold sails in, sometimes you need to be able to hold a sail out, as in running before the wind. A sail with a boom will stay out of its own accord pretty well, but if you are sailing really dead before the wind, perhaps with sails wing-and-wing, or if the boat is rolling a lot, then the danger of jibing is real, and jibing needs to be prevented. So you rig a preventer on your boom. It's simply a line leading forward from the outboard end of the boom and belayed as far forward as is practical. It needs to be heavier than the sheet, because it is only a single part and will take a heavy strain should the sail get aback. Make the preventer fast to an eye at the end of the boom with a buntline hitch, or around the end of the boom with a clove hitch backed by a half hitch, lead it forward outside the lee shrouds, and take it through some fairlead well forward, and then to belay. A bow chock is often a good fairlead for a preventer, and an anchor cleat, post, or bitt is often a convenient belaying point. If you have a bowsprit, by all means lead the preventer to the outboard end of it; the further forward you can lead the preventer, the more forward the angle of pull on the boom. You may want to put a single block at the bowsprit end specifically to take your preventer. This is a good place for an open snatch block that will take the bight of a line. You don't need purchase on a preventer, because you can set it up with the boom's sheet eased off a bit extra and then use the purchase of the sheet to haul the boom back taut against the preventer. But take it easy, because you are pulling with considerable power against the single-part preventer.

Rigging a Boom Vang

A sheet not only trims a sail in, to control its angle to the wind, but also down, which reduces the twist in the sail, though the downward effect decreases markedly as the sheet is eased and the boat is sailed farther off the wind. As you ease the sheet and head off on a broad reach or run, if there's much strength in the wind, the boom lifts, allowing the head of the sail to twist off to leeward. Not only does the sail lose its shape and driving force, but you can't slack the sheet off as far as you'd like to to square the boom off, because then the upper part of the sail will chafe too much against the lee shrouds. To hold the boom down when the sheet is eased, you can rig a boom vang, a short piece of rigging attached to the boom about half the boat's beam aft of the gooseneck and made fast on the lee rail at a point that will lead it down as vertically as possible. The vang needs to pull down hard on its boom to do its job, so it needs to be plenty strong, at least as strong as the sheet.

Here's a good quick way to rig a boom vang. Use a heavy piece of line about three times as long as the distance that will be covered by the vang from the boom to the eye fitting on the lee rail. Reeve the end through the rail fitting, and tie a bowline in it. Take the other end of the line to the boom, take the slack out of the line, and tie the line around the boom with a clove hitch backed by a half hitch or to a fitting on the boom with a bunt-line hitch. (Here's a good place to use a bight of the line as if it were an end, so you don't have to pull the long end of the line through when you tie the line to the boom.) Reeve the long end left over through the bowline at the rail. You have a crude but effective two-part tackle. Cinch the vang up tight by hauling on the end rove through the bowline, and make it fast by tying the vang off at the bow-line with three half hitches. Make up the vang this way with the sheet eased off a bit extra and then haul back against the vang with the sheet. This sort of vang is a bit makeshift in that when you jibe, it has to be let go from the lee rail before the jibe and then set up again on the other side after the jibe.

A lee running backstay tackle (never in use on the lee side when you are sailing off the wind) may be in a good position to double as a boom vang. If you connect your backstay tackles to their stays with snap shackles, you can quickly disconnect the leeward one, take the stay forward to be held by a snaphook seized to the lee, aftermost shroud, and now you have a tackle ready to snap into a fitting on the boom so it can become a boom vang, the hauling part leading aft to its accustomed cleat. Using the same tackle for two distinct functions that can never interfere with each other is very satisfying.

A good way to set up a permanent boom vang is to rig a heavy tackle leading from the vang point on the boom to a point on deck a little abaft the mast on the centerline. Being on the centerline gives the vang a less advantageous angle of pull (less vertical), but means you don't have to attend to it when jibing. Having the vang be a tackle, instead of what amounts to a two-part lashing as described above for the makeshift vang, means you can trim the sheet and then haul on the vang until you get the boom

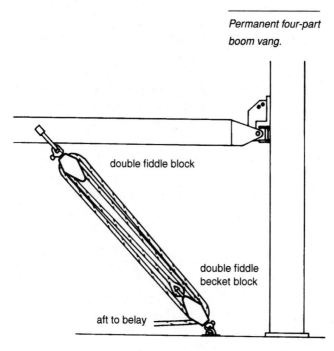

Permanent four-part boom vang.

double fiddle block

double fiddle becket block

aft to belay

down where you want it, or until you don't dare haul on it any more for fear of something carrying away. The boom vang tackle should be of four parts, with the hauling part coming off the lower block and leading aft to a convenient belaying point, so use a double becket block for the lower block and a double block for the upper block. This is a good place to use fiddle blocks (their shells are shaped like fiddles) with sheaves tangential instead of concentric, because they tend to resist twist in the tackle more than normal blocks.

Poling Out a Headsail

A sail with no boom, like a headsail, needs a pole to hold it out when running before the wind. One end of the pole is secured to the mast, and the other end to the clew of the sail. If the boat has a spinnaker pole, that is ideal; it has its own fitting on the mast to hold the inboard end in a universal joint. Otherwise, you can lash a pole to the mast with a stout rope lanyard, known in this application as a *snotter*. Tie one end of the snotter around the pole near its inboard end with a rolling hitch, worked up really tight and backed by a half hitch or two. Tie the other end, hauled taut, to an eye fitting several feet up the mast with two or three half hitches—or again, tie the snotter right around the mast with a good, tight rolling hitch backed by half hitches. A spinnaker pole will have an eye in its outer end closed by a spring-loaded pin, and this eye can go right on the sail's sheet at the clew to hold the pole to the sail. Otherwise, you can take a clove hitch around the end of the pole with the slack lee sheet of the sail to hold the pole to the sail's clew. Then rig a preventer on a headsail pole, just as you would on a boom.

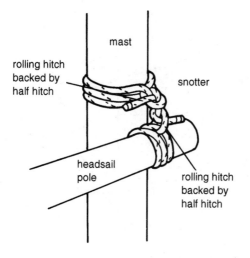

mast

rolling hitch
backed by
half hitch

snotter

headsail
pole

rolling hitch
backed by
half hitch

If you find yourself rigging a pole for a headsail often, or if you need to pole out a headsail with an area of 300 square feet or more, then it will be a good idea to have a pole that is handy to secure to the mast and that can be set up independently of the sail (that is, not depend on the sail itself and its sheet for support), so you can set the pole in the desired position and then haul the clew of the headsail out to its outboard end. A spinnaker pole, with its mast fitting, topping lift, and forward and after guys, fills the bill nicely, and is well worth having along to pole out jibs even though you may not contemplate setting a spinnaker. Otherwise, you can rig a topping lift and guys on any pole. For the topping lift, it may be most convenient to use a spare headsail halyard, if available, shackling the halyard into an eye fitting on the end of the pole. Otherwise, you can rig a single-part whip aloft for a topping lift.

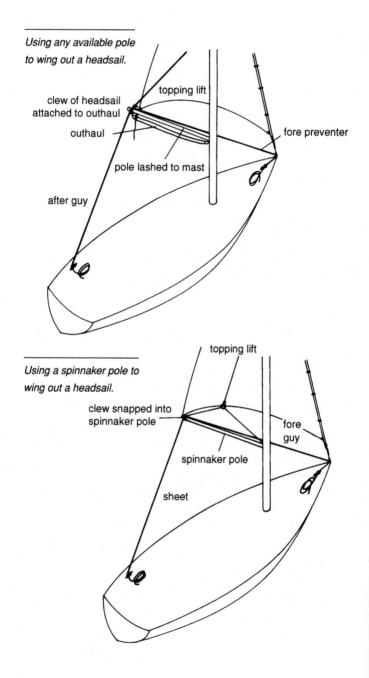

Using any available pole to wing out a headsail.

topping lift

clew of headsail attached to outhaul

outhaul

fore preventer

pole lashed to mast

after guy

Using a spinnaker pole to wing out a headsail.

topping lift

clew snapped into spinnaker pole

fore guy

spinnaker pole

sheet

Dead-end the lift at an eye fitting on the outboard end of the pole with a buntline hitch, lead it aloft through a single block on the forward side of the mast about halfway up, and down to belay on the mast. The pole should be light enough that you won't need purchase on the lift. The forward guy you already have as a preventer. The after guy you can rig simply with a line secured to the outer end of the pole with a clove hitch backed by a half hitch and led aft through a fairlead or lead block as far aft as practical, and to belay. Now you have a pole supported at the mast and with its outer end held up, held forward and down, and held aft and down, and the three lines to the outboard end of the pole can all be adjusted to put the pole exactly where you want it.

All that remains is to rig an outhaul on the pole so that, once you get the pole set up, you can haul the clew of the sail out to the end of it. Secure a single block at the outer end of the pole, reeve a line through it, and tie its ends together with a square knot at the inboard end of the pole, leaving enough of the ends to be able to tie them through the clew of the headsail with another square knot. Belay either part of this outhaul to a cleat on the pole at its inboard end. Now you can haul the sail's clew out to the end of the pole and back in again with the pole in place.

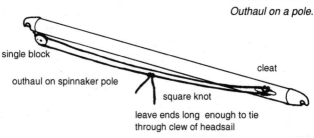

Outhaul on a pole.

single block

cleat

outhaul on spinnaker pole

square knot

leave ends long enough to tie
through clew of headsail

Poling Out a Dinghy

To keep the dinghy from going bump in the night, you can rig a boat boom exactly as you would rig a pole for a big headsail. Instead of holding out the clew of a headsail, the boat boom holds out the small boat. Just make the boat's painter fast to the outhaul on the boom. Now you can haul the dinghy in to embark in her and, when you come back on board, haul her out to where you can forget about her no matter what the caprices of wind and tide.

Poling out a dinghy.

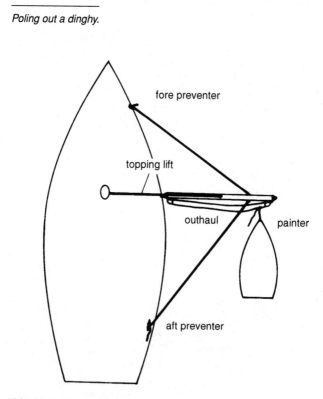

Lashing Down the Tiller

To lash a tiller in place, when conditions of wind and sea are steady enough so the boat will steer herself, use a buntline hitch to dead-end a small, cable-laid line to a convenient fitting abreast the end of the tiller, and make the line fast to the end of the tiller with a clove hitch. Adjust this tiller line to exactly where you want it by taking off the second half hitch of the clove hitch, making your adjustment with the first half hitch, and then putting the second half hitch back on. If you are lashing the tiller hard down when hove to (when no adjustment will be necessary), back the clove hitch with a half hitch. Lash a wheel the same way, with the wheel rope clove-hitched around a spoke. To keep the wheel from kicking, tie on a second wheel rope from the opposite side as well.

14 Shortening Sail

When the wind blows hard, it's time to shorten sail. When the boat starts to struggle a bit, maybe heeling over too far with the lee rail going under in the gusts, and people start looking anxious, then you reef the mainsail (or other sails), and the effect is marvelous. Despite the fact that it's breezing up with a correspondingly rougher sea, the boat regains her easy motion, she gets back on her feet, her people relax again, and frowns are replaced by smiles. And for the sailor, there's something wonderful about watching a boat go through rough water in a strong breeze, her sails made modest through reefing.

When rigging or using reefing gear, remember bending sail, because what you are doing in reefing is simply slacking the halyard and giving the sail a new foot, partway up its height. Securing the new foot to the boom is just like attaching the foot of the sail to the boom when you bent on the sail.

The necessary hardware for putting in a reef consists of a luff cringle, a leech cringle, and a row of either reef points or grommets across the sail between them. First, lash down the luff cringle at the gooseneck in the position where you want it when the sail is set. Make a simple lashing around the gooseneck, two turns and a square knot. Have a heavy lanyard for this luff earing, as it's called, and don't be tempted to use it for anything else, like lashing down the anchor, or else it may be unavailable just when you really need it to reef. I heard of one skipper who kept his reefing earings under his pillow so he'd always know right where to find them.

If you'd like to make up a permanent luff earing, take a short piece of strong rope, tie it into an eye fitting low down on one side of the mast with a buntline hitch, or splice it into the eye with an eye splice, and have a cleat for it low down on the other side of the mast. Make the earing long enough to go up through the luff reefing cringle and back down to its cleat. Since the earing is only two parts, it should be about as heavy a line as will easily reeve through the cringle. This rig makes a very quick and easy way to lash down the luff reefing cringle and, best of all, since the earing lives on the mast, it's always there when you need it. Now, if you give this luff earing extra length, so it can reeve up through the halyard fitting on the head of the sail when the sail is furled, you'll have a handy way

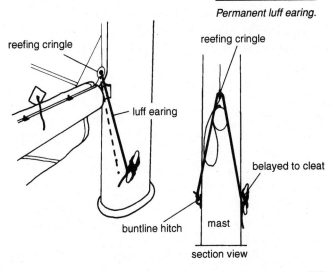

Permanent luff earing.

reefing cringle

reefing cringle

luff earing

belayed to cleat

buntline hitch   mast

section view

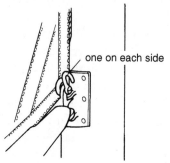

Inverted hooks at the gooseneck.

one on each side

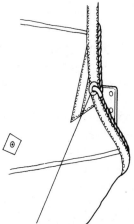

when reefing, feed luff cringle onto windward hook

to tie down the head of the sail as soon as it is lowered (see also page 92). An even quicker way to secure the luff reefing cringle at the gooseneck makes use of a special fitting consisting of a pair of inverted hooks, one on each side of the gooseneck. You simply feed the luff cringle onto the windward hook, which will then hold the cringle down in the right position.

I prefer the permanent earing, because with it you can adjust the position of the luff cringle to a nicety, and when shaking the reef, you can let it go without touching the halyard (which you must ease before you can get the cringle off the reefing hook).

The leech reefing cringle must be hauled aft, like an outhaul, to stretch the new foot of the reefed sail taut along the boom, and it also must hold down to the boom the leech cringle, which becomes the clew of the reefed sail. If no leech earing exists, these goals can be achieved with a simple lashing. Reeve a fairly long, stout line through an eye fitting on the after end of the boom to its middle, lead both ends back forward, and reeve them through the leech reefing cringle in opposite directions. Now haul aft hard on both ends. Because you are pulling on two hauling parts, you have two makeshift tackles, each using the leech cringle as a block, giving you purchase. When you have hauled aft enough to stretch the foot of the sail taut (usually this means pulling on the earing about as hard as you can), take the ends of the earing down around the sail and boom right at the leech reefing cringle, with the ends going around in opposite directions. Go around again with each end going the opposite way. Then tie off the ends with a triple square knot.

Rigging a permanent leech reefing earing that lives on the boom like an outhaul makes a much easier job of

Reefing the mainsail clew with a temporary leech earing. Reeve a stout lanyard through a boom-end eye, then lead the ends forward, reeving them through the leech reefing cringle from opposite sides. Haul the clew aft, then wrap the ends twice around the boom in opposite directions, finishing with a triple square knot.

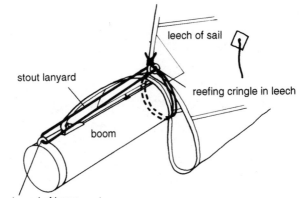

leech of sail

stout lanyard

reefing cringle in leech

boom

eye in end of boom

hauling out the foot of the sail when reefing. Dead-end the leech earing with a buntline hitch tied into an eye fitting positioned on one side of the boom just abaft the point where the leech reefing cringle will come when the foot of the sail is stretched taut for the reef. Lead the earing up through the leech reefing cringle and back down through a single cheek block on the opposite side of the boom right across from the eye fitting, then forward to belay on a cleat on the side of the boom, well forward so it will be easy to reach even with the boom broad off. This rig gives a crude, two-part purchase, using the leech reefing cringle as a "block." Add purchase to this leech earing using the same methods for various sizes of sails as described on page 84 for outhauls. Have your outhaul tackle on one side of the boom and your leech earing tackle on the other.

Now you have the reef's luff and leech secured, corresponding to the sail's tack and clew. To secure the foot of the reef to the boom, tie in the reef points. Pass each leeward reef point through between the sail and boom, haul taut, and tie it to the corresponding windward reef point with—what else?—the reef, or square, knot. Leave

---

Permanent leech earing.

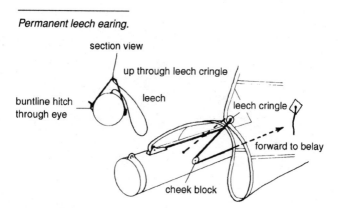

section view

up through leech cringle

buntline hitch
through eye

leech

leech cringle

forward to belay

cheek block

the longer end (the windward reef point) not pulled through, to form a sort of half bow that will be very easy to untie when you go to shake out the reef. As you haul each reef point taut, try to get an even strain among the points. When you have tied them all, go back and check that each is around the foot of the sail only (no rigging tied in with them) and that, on a sail with more than one reef, the reef points you tied all actually belong to the reef you want.

If the foot of the sail is held to the boom by slides in an internal track, then you can't have reef points, because you can't pass them between the sail and boom. In this case, you'll have grommets in the sail instead of reef points, but don't be tempted to pass individual sail stops through them and around the boom; the uneven pressure on the stops could rip the sail. Instead, to secure the foot of the reef to the boom, spiral a laceline through the grommets just as if you were bending sail (see page 85). Reef points are much handier to work than lacelines.

If you want to be able to sail in heavy weather, you'll need a second reef, above the first, in order to shorten sail

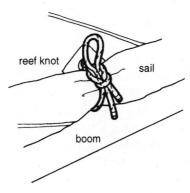

Tying reef points.

still further. And in a mainsail as big as, say, 300 square feet, you'll want a third reef. These will, of course, have their own cringles and reef points. The best rig is to have a permanent luff earing, which you can use for any reef. As to the leech earing, you have the choice, for second and third reefs, of rigging permanent earings and living with all that line hanging from the sail, or reeving off the earing only when you need it, a time-consuming and sometimes dangerous chore. My choice is to live with permanent leech earings and know that reefing will always be relatively quick and easy.

Tying in a Reef

Here's a step-by-step outline of the procedure for tying in a reef and then shaking it out. To reef, ease the sheet until much of the sail is luffing; set up the topping lift to take the weight of the boom; slack the halyard until the luff reefing cringle is just below the gooseneck; secure the luff cringle; haul out the leech earing; tie the reef points or reeve the laceline, trimming the sheet in as necessary to reach the after part of the sail; check the reef points or laceline; ease the sheet back out; hoist away on the halyard; ease the topping lift; and trim the sheet to where you want it.

To shake out a reef, let go the reef points or unreeve the laceline from aft to forward; ease the sheet until the sail is luffing; take the weight of the boom on the topping lift; slack the leech earing; let go the luff earing; hoist away on the halyard; slack the topping lift; and trim the sheet. Somehow, seeing the full sail set again in moderating conditions carries an equal satisfaction to reefing.

Roller Reefing Systems

I guess I should say a few words about roller reefing, although there's a minimum of ropework involved with the various systems and little choice about how to rig them. For boomed sails, there are systems that roll the foot of the sail around the boom, that roll the foot of the sail up inside the boom, and that roll the luff of the sail up on a wire, usually inside the mast, but sometimes immediately abaft the mast. All involve mechanical or rope-to-drum connections to do the rotating. The last two serve as furling systems as well as reefing systems. The last one requires that the sail be loose-footed, instead of having the sail's foot attached to the boom, and it needs a very strong outhaul to haul the clew out along the boom and hold it in the desired position. Then, for boomless sails, like jibs, there are roller furling systems that will roll the sail up around a luff wire or extruded foil at the luff, and some of these, especially the foil systems when used with a working jib, as opposed to a genoa jib, work quite well for reefing. The key to reefing a headsail with roller furling gear is that the sail needs to be narrow enough—that is, have a short enough foot—so it doesn't have a chance to get baggy in the middle when you roll it partway up.

Have any of these systems and their associated furling lines plenty strong, for in heavy weather they will be asked to take extremely heavy strains at times. For instance, if you are going to use a roller foil headsail system to carry a working jib reefed down in heavy weather, there will be a heavy strain on the furling line keeping the sail rolled partway up, and if it parts, you'll suddenly have a lot more sail than you want just when you want it least. The great advantages to all these systems are that they make extremely quick and easy work of reefing and furling and that they permit infinite adjustments of sail area. The big drawback is that they depend on sophisticated fittings, some of which are hard to reach when something goes wrong and most of which are hard to repair on board, fittings which, if they fail, can land you in rather a mess with sails that perhaps cannot be set, or, worse yet, cannot be taken in. Generally speaking, even the best roller reefing systems do so at some sacrifice to sail shape.

Trysails

When it blows a gale, it pays to have deep reefs in your sails, and if it blows so hard that even a close-reefed mainsail presents too much area to the wind, then the thing to have to be able to keep going, or, perhaps, to heave to, is a trysail. It's a small, heavy, triangular sail—a tiny, bulletproof sort of sail—about half the size of your close-reefed mainsail, or, say, about one-sixth the size of the full mainsail. The trysail should be short on the luff with the tack set well above the gooseneck to keep the forward part of the sail out of a sea breaking over the boat. The foot should be quite long and slope downward from forward to aft, so the clew will come only a bit higher than the foot of the mainsail. Shaped in this way (the sail is loose-footed, of course), the trysail clew can be lashed to the main boom, which is lifted a bit on its topping lift, and then you can trim the trysail with the mainsheet. Before setting the trysail, you would, of course, furl the mainsail very securely on its boom; this is a good time to use that stout furling line with marling hitches (see page 91).

Here's a good way to rig a trysail. Have a stout, four-part tackle made up and shackled to the tack cringle (double upper block, single becket lower block) for a tack downhaul. Shackle the lower block to an eye fitting on one side of the gooseneck, overhaul the tackle to give it a bit more than enough length to allow the tack of the trysail to be hoisted into position, and belay the downhaul to a cleat on the other side of the mast. Feed the trysail luff slides onto the track on the mast. A gate in the track above the furled mainsail is essential. Even better, if you are doing much sailing in heavy weather, is a separate track for the trysail, beside the mainsail track, so you can leave the trysail bent on when the mainsail is set. Shackle the main halyard into the head of the trysail. Stretch the trysail's foot out taut, and lash the clew of the trysail to the boom, passing

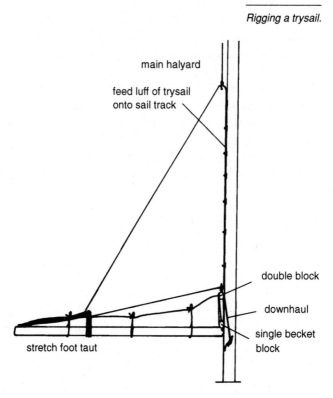

Rigging a trysail.

main halyard

feed luff of trysail
onto sail track

double block

downhaul

single becket
block

stretch foot taut

the lashing around mainsail and boom using the same lashing as described for a leech reefing earing on page 130. The clew cringle of the trysail ought to be big enough so this lashing can be of really strong rope, at least ½ inch for a trysail of 75 square feet. Now she's ready to hoist. Hoist the sail smartly, haul down the tack hard, adjust the topping lift, if necessary, and trim the sheet. Set the trysail often enough in moderate weather so it will be a familiar process to you in heavy weather.

Many sailors associate the trysail only with offshore cruising boats, but it is an excellent sail for coastwise cruising as well, making it possible to take advantage of a fair wind in heavy weather. It is even an excellent sail for a small daysailer, enabling her to venture out in a strong breeze or even perhaps a gale in protected water. I rigged a tiny little thing on a 14-foot open sailing dinghy and used it with great pleasure a couple of times to sail around in the harbor on days when there were some really heavy gusts. You had to be quick on your toes when they hit, but the little boat, with her triangular handkerchief set, was no more in danger of capsizing than she would have been under full sail in a moderate but puffy breeze.

15 Gaff Rig

Despite the gaff rig's being out of vogue these days, it does have merit for cruising, and you still see a few gaff-rigged cruising boats. The chief difference between the gaff rig and the Marconi is that the gaff rig is much less lofty, so that a gaff sail of the same area as a Marconi sail exerts less heeling force on the boat. That can be a distinct advantage to a cruising boat with a relatively low ballast-to-displacement ratio. The gaff sail is more efficient off the wind (holds the wind better), and the Marconi sail is more efficient on the wind (holds the wind at a sharper angle to the wind and gives more lift). The gaff rig has an extra spar and two halyards instead of one (though the mast and standing rigging of a Marconi rig are more complicated and expensive). The gaff sail takes a bit longer to reef, with its longer foot. If you have to go to the masthead, you appreciate the shorter mast of a gaff rig. Finally, as a sailor, you spend a lot of time watching your sails, and the four-sided gaff sail is far more interesting to watch, at least to me, than the mere triangle of a Marconi sail. Anyway, I think enough of the gaff rig (actually, I'm quite partial to it) to include here a discussion of its rigging.

Bending and Hoisting Sail

The gaff is the spar that stretches and supports the head of the sail. Its forward end slides on the mast, held to the mast by jaws. The jaws are kept from coming off the mast by a line between the ends of the jaws called a parrel line. A good way to rig a parrel line is simply to bore holes in the ends of the jaws and run a light line through them, held by a figure-eight knot on the outside of each jaw. Leave enough slack in the parrel line so it won't quite come taut when the gaff is peaked up. If you want to get fancy, you can string wooden parrel beads on your parrel line to reduce friction and chafe.

With gaff rig, wooden mast hoops are the traditional—and utterly practical—way of holding the sail to its spar (you see ads for them in the backs of magazines about traditional boats). To bend on sail using mast

Attaching the gaff.

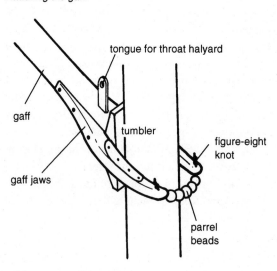

tongue for throat halyard

gaff

gaff jaws

tumbler

figure-eight knot

parrel beads

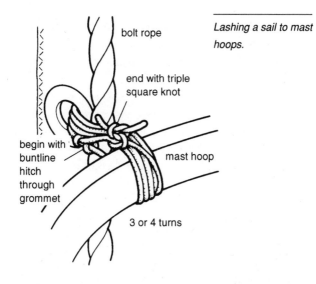

bolt rope

end with triple
square knot

*Lashing a sail to mast
hoops.*

begin with
buntline
hitch
through
grommet

mast hoop

3 or 4 turns

hoops, you lash each hoop to its corresponding grommet
in the luff of the sail (small, braided polyester does the
job well). Tie the end of the lashing into the grommet with
a buntline hitch, leaving three or four inches of end. Pass
the other end of the lashing around the masthoop and
through the grommet to take three or four turns, then tie
to the end you left using a square knot with at least three
over hands.

You rig two halyards on your gaff, a throat halyard on
its forward end and a peak halyard on its after end. Both
halyards should have the same amount of purchase so that,
except on a big sail, one sailor can hoist away on both halyards at once (if he's been clever enough to lead them
down the same side of the mast), and both ends of the
gaff will go up at the same speed. The way to set a gaff
sail is to hoist the gaff horizontally until the luff comes
taut, belay the peak halyard momentarily, set the luff up
hard with the throat halyard, and then set up the peak
halyard until you get some wrinkles from peak to tack—

the harder it's blowing, the more wrinkles. These wrinkles smooth out when the sail fills. A gaff sail whose peak isn't set up quite high enough just doesn't look right and loses efficiency to windward.

On a small craft with a sail of, say, no more than 100 square feet and a light gaff, a two-part purchase is enough for each halyard. The throat halyard dead-ends with a buntline hitch on a becket block a foot above where the gaff jaws come on the mast when the sail is set. Then it

Two-part halyards.

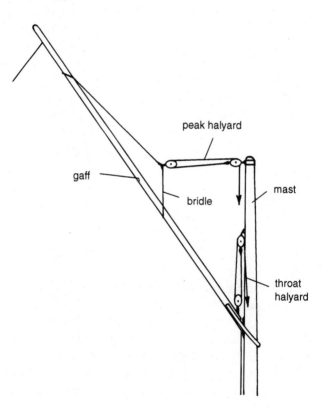

peak halyard

gaff

bridle

mast

throat
halyard

leads down through a single block secured to the top of the forward end of the gaff (shackled into a metal tongue), back aloft through the becket block and down to belay. The peak halyard dead-ends with a buntline hitch on a becket block positioned at the masthead, leads down through a single block on a bridle on the gaff, from forward to aft, back up through the becket block, from aft to forward, and down to belay.

The bridle is a span of rope or wire along the top of the gaff. Its purpose is to spread the strain of the halyard along the gaff. If the peak halyard were attached directly to the gaff, it would be attached about three quarters of the length of the gaff from its forward end. The bridle is attached to the gaff so as to span this point. Each end of the bridle is spliced, with an eye splice, right round the gaff, with wooden shoulders, or cleats (not the sort of cleats you belay to, more like the cleats on soccer shoes), to keep the ends from sliding together along the spar. In a small craft, the bridle may be of rope, three times as strong as the halyard. In a bigger boat, strength requirements usually dictate that the bridle be of wire. The lower peak halyard block can be attached to the bridle by using a becket block and simply running the bridle through the becket before splicing the bridle to the gaff. A special fitting used to be made for the purpose. It's a block with a bronze saddle secured to its lower end, a saddle designed to take the wire bridle of a gaff. The bridle is secured in the saddle by a fitting that closes the top of the saddle and is held in place by two spring-loaded pins. With this fitting, the lower peak halyard block can be removed easily from the bridle, as when you want to set an awning over the sail. It's worth trying to find one of these special peak halyard blocks in the odds-and-ends department of a boatyard.

On a gaff sail with an area of 100 square feet to 500 square feet, you need three-part halyards. On the throat

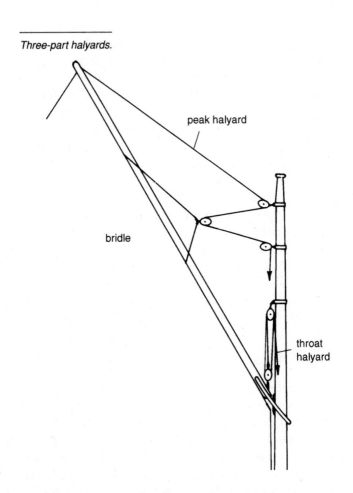

Three-part halyards.

peak halyard

bridle

throat halyard

halyard, the lower block would be a becket block, and the upper a double block. The three-part peak halyard would be rigged with a dead-end near the end of the gaff (tie to an eye-bolt with the buntline hitch), up through a single block at the masthead, down through a single block on a bridle, back aloft through another single block a foot or two below the upper block, and down to belay. The lead through all these blocks is from aft to forward.

These three-part halyards leave you considerable rope to coil down after your gaff sail is set. This is where belaying pins in a fife rail or pin rail come into their own, because belaying pins will hold your coils much better than will mere cleats.

The Gaff Vang

Now we come to one of my favorite pieces of rigging, the gaff vang. It's a line made fast to the end of the gaff (with, say, a buntline hitch on an eye-bolt, with its eye on the underside of the gaff), used to trim or control the gaff. A gaff sail twists more than a Marconi sail, because the gaff itself makes the head of the sail sag off to leeward. This ill can be cured with a vang. If the gaff sail is the aftermost sail in the boat, as in a sloop or cutter or the mainsail of a schooner, then the vang leads straight down to the deck, where it can belay, say, to a quarter bitt on the weather side. It has to be let go before a tack and particularly before a jibe and then set up again to windward. If the boom overhangs the stern, as it usually does with gaff rig, then you need two vangs, one on each side, to save the difficult job it would be to pass a vang around the end of the boom. With two vangs, the leeward one, not in use, is simply taken forward and belayed, with the slack out but no strain on it, so as not to interfere with the curvature of the sail, at a convenient point in the lee shrouds, or at the foot of the mast, or, say, on a belaying pin in the side of the boom jaws. Don't belay a vang leading from aloft directly to a deck cleat. The cleat wasn't designed to be pulled up on. Instead, lead the vang through a lead block on deck and then along the deck to the cleat.

If you are lucky enough to have a mast abaft your gaff sail, as with the gaff mainsail of a ketch or yawl, or the

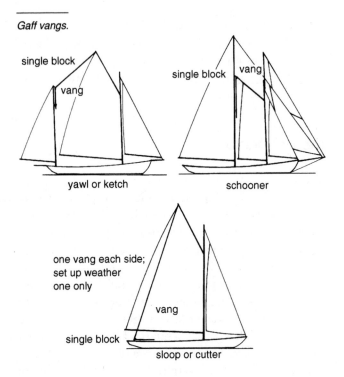

Gaff vangs.

single block
vang
yawl or ketch

single block
vang
schooner

one vang each side;
set up weather
one only
vang
single block
sloop or cutter

gaff foresail of a schooner, then by all means lead your vang through a single block on that mast and down to belay to a cleat on that mast. This rig improves greatly the lead of the vang, letting it pull aft more than down. A drawback to the vang led to an after mast is that it cannot be used to haul down on the gaff when taking in the sail, as can a vang led straight to the deck.

Rigging a Preventer Backstay

A preventer backstay is a wonderful thing to have at times, the thing prevented being the loss of your mast. Most

Marconi-rigged boats come equipped with permanent backstays, but the opposite is true for gaff rig. My tiny, gaff-rigged schooner was designed with just a springstay between the mastheads and a single, aft-leading shroud on each side to hold up her mainmast, which was stepped atop the centerboard trunk. Obviously, if any one of these three wires were to part, down would tumble the mainmast. Being something of a pessimist, I doubled up on the springstay and added a preventer backstay on each side, leading down a bit aft of the shrouds and made up with a simple lashing between an eye on the lower end of the backstay and an eye on deck. The lee one had to be slacked when off the wind, of course, but was far enough forward so it could be left set up when close hauled. One of these backstays—set up, luckily, just as one of the fittings holding a shroud let go—on one occasion saved the mast.

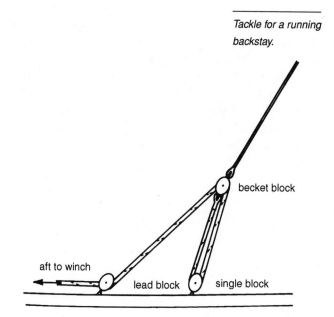

Tackle for a running backstay.

becket block

aft to winch

lead block

single block

Although this chapter is primarily about gaff rig, it's worth considering rigging preventer backstays even on a modern rig to give your mast extra support in heavy weather or when you may want to drive her a bit in more moderate weather.

The key to rigging a tackle for a running backstay is to spread out its lower blocks fore and aft along the deck to keep the tackle from twisting. You'll want a minimum purchase of three parts, with an upper becket block, lower single block on deck forward, and lead block aft, with the tail, or fall of the tackle, leading aft. If you have winches for the jibsheets, you can use the windward one to help set up the backstay. Otherwise, if you need more purchase, you can clap another tackle onto the fall of the backstay tackle, as described for outhauls on page 84.

A handy rig on a running backstay is a light line tied with a buntline hitch into the lower eye of the backstay (just above the upper block of the tackle), leading forward through a single block about six feet up on the lee shroud, and aft to belay. When you let go the lee backstay, you can haul in on this line and it will haul the backstay forward out of the way (overhauling the tackle) and hold it to the lee shroud. With this rig, you need quite a long fall on the backstay tackle, but it's worth it.

For another way to secure the lee backstay and, in fact, a way to use it for a boom vang, see page 120.

16   Holding the Boat

Anchoring

The biggest, and in some ways the most important, piece of rope you have in your boat is the anchor line, or rode. For any boat up to about 35 feet long, the anchor rode should be at least ⅝ inch. Bigger boats should use even heavier rope. You want not only strength, but also extra diameter in case of chafe. As mentioned previously, the best rope for an anchor rode is cable-laid polyester or nylon. Any anchor rode in a cruising boat should be no less than 300 feet long. Period. Sometimes there is just no substitute for plenty of scope.

It's a good idea to combine a length of chain with your anchor rode. Ten or 20 feet of chain next to the anchor will help it hold because of the chain's weight, will prevent the line from chafing off against anything sharp on the bottom, and will keep the line a bit freer of sand and mud, which will soil and deteriorate it. Use ⅜-inch chain on boats up to 35 feet long; heavier for bigger boats. Galvanized "High Test" chain is best, but be sure to match the chain link to your windlass wildcat, the turning part on one end specially shaped to grip chain. Some sailors like an all-chain anchor rode. It's chafe-proof, strong, and its heavy catenary provides "elasticity."

For an all-chain anchor cable, it helps to use a strong (anchor-line-sized) nylon snubber as a sort of rubber band between chain and boat, so if she pitches and yanks hard on the chain and it straightens out (loses its catenary), there won't be a fearful jerk that could part the chain, damage a fitting, or break out the anchor. Here's a good way to rig such a snubber: Put an eye splice around a thimble in the outboard end of the snubber, and put a shackle on the thimble whose pin will just fit through a link of the chain. Make the snubber about 30 feet long, and whip the end. You're in business. When you anchor and have veered almost the amount of chain you want, shackle the snubber into the chain, make the end fast as you would an anchor rode, and veer more chain until the chain goes slack and the strain comes on the snubber. Of course you secure the chain in its slack position in case the snubber should part. To weigh anchor, simply heave in on the chain until the snubber shackle is within reach, unshackle it, and continue as you would ordinarily.

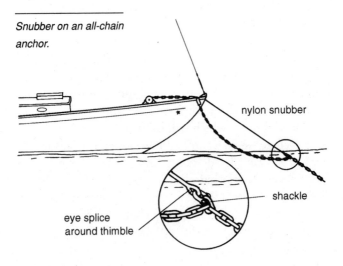

Snubber on an all-chain anchor.

nylon snubber

shackle

eye splice around thimble

Securing the Anchor Rode

To secure the anchor rode to the anchor, use the anchor bend for tying an anchor rode directly to the ring of an anchor, or an eye splice around a thimble to take a shackle to connect the rode to the anchor ring or to a length of chain. Of course, chain would be shackled to the anchor. Secure the screw pins of any shackles used on the anchor rode with wire so they can't untwist.

The fitting to which you belay the anchor rode deserves special attention. At times, it will be asked to take heavy, perhaps even jolting, strains. First off, there should be two such fittings, one for each anchor rode for the times when you are anchoring with two anchors. It's hard to adjust two heavily straining anchor rodes to a nicety if each doesn't have its own cleat or bitt.

A bitt, or samson post, makes the best and strongest fitting for belaying an anchor rode. It is simply a heavy metal or wooden post with a heavy metal pin crossing through the top of it. Have two of them. Use the tow-boat hitch on them. Large, heavy cleats also work well for the anchor rodes. In any case, make sure the fittings to which the anchor rodes are belayed are plenty strong— through-bolted, or preferably, attached to structural members of the hull.

A good way to secure the bitter end of the anchor rode to the vessel, so it can't go overboard if you get too enthu- siastic about veering scope (how embarrassing!) or if you want more security for the anchor rode in a hard gale or— perish the thought—hurricane, is to tie the end of the anchor rode to the foot of the mast with a round turn and two half hitches (might as well use up the end and make three or four half hitches). If your mast steps on deck, don't tie the bitter end of the anchor rode to it, because the fitting that holds the foot of the mast wasn't designed to take a heavy strain from forward.

Trip Lines and Spring Lines

Rig a trip line on your anchor when over foul bottom (jagged rocks, old automobiles, etc.) to give yourself a good chance of recovering your anchor should it hook somebody's bumper. It's simply a line, nearly as strong as the anchor rode, made fast to the crown of the anchor with a buntline hitch, long enough to more than reach the surface at high tide, and with a buoy on it. (The buoyed trip line also lets other sailors know where your anchor is.) Should the anchor foul some obstruction on the bottom, you can pick up the trip line and pull on the crown of the anchor, which will probably free it.

My last anchor tip is right out of Hornblower. When C. S. Forester's hero, at anchor, wanted to be able to

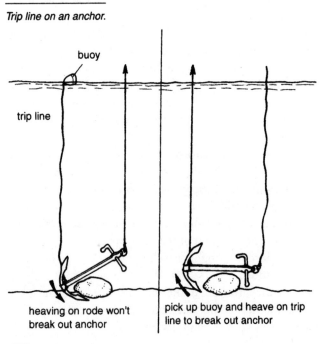

Trip line on an anchor.

buoy

trip line

heaving on rode won't break out anchor

pick up buoy and heave on trip line to break out anchor

maneuver his ship so as to bring his broadside to bear on the enemy, he would remark to his first lieutenant, "I'll have a spring on the cable, if you please, Mr. Bush." Mr. Bush would, of course, oblige, and then Hornblower's man o'war was ready to turn herself in any desired direction while at anchor. You can do the same thing in order to bring a light breeze across the cockpit on a hot day, head your boat into a nasty swell that's making her roll unconscionably, or bring your own broadside to bear.

Belay a stout line about three times as long as your boat to the anchor rode, outboard of its chock, with a rolling hitch backed by a half hitch. Take the other end of the line aft on the side of the boat you want to be to windward, outboard of all rigging, and lead it through a stern chock to belay on a quarter bitt or stern cleat. Now, by merely slacking the anchor rode (assuming there's enough wind to put a strain on it), you can turn the boat, for the spring you led aft will begin to take some of the strain on the anchor and will begin to swing her stern towards the anchor. The more anchor rode you veer, the more strain comes on the spring, and the more she swings her stern up into the wind. Veer anchor rode equal to the length of the spring, and she'll lie with wind abeam. Veer anchor rode until it's slack, and she'll lie entirely to the spring, stern to wind. This maneuvering takes a bit of swinging room, of course, and so isn't possible in a crowded anchorage. It also may put a greater strain on the anchor rode, as when you turn the boat to bring the wind abeam. I used a spring on my cable recently to great advantage. I was anchored in a deserted West Indian cove, the trade wind blowing out of the east as usual and a disturbing little surge coming in from the south, making the boat roll most uncomfortably. I put a spring on my cable and swung her bow into the swell. Ah, just a gentle pitching. This simple trick turned an all-but-untenable anchorage into a pleasant one.

Docking

Dock lines should be 75 percent as strong as the anchor rode, be about one and a half times the length of the boat, be four in number, and be available without undue unloading of lockers. Have them rigged and ready to go before you make your landing alongside, bow line and forward spring on the foredeck, stern line and after spring on the stern. Tie a big (three-foot loop) bowline in the outboard end of each—that way, you'll be absolutely certain your dock lines will fit over whatever pilings may present themselves. Make the inboard ends of the dock lines fast to their posts or cleats. Lead them out through their chocks, and then coil them carefully to the bowlines, so they're ready to heave without kinks (see pages 47 and 48).

For throwing dock lines when landing, also see pages 47 and 48. But maybe your skipper can get you almost but not quite close enough to pass a dock line's bowline over a piling (as often happens when tying up in a marina).

Dock line placement.

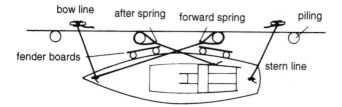

Rather than try to toss it over the piling, rest the loop of the bowline on the back side of your boat hook and use the length of the boat hook to extend your reach. This technique becomes especially handy when you have to pass the bowline of a dock line over a high piling (at low tide) or a high bollard (in a canal lock when going up).

When handling dock lines, look to the person with the con (usually at the helm) for instructions on slacking, checking (slacking under strain), or holding. Make safety your first thought. Watch your fingers; don't use body parts for fenders; get out of the line of fire of dock lines that may part (see page 4). When checking, or, especially holding, use plenty of turns.

If you're about to get underway from a dock, and the usual dockside loafers have made themselves scarce, lead the last dock lines you will cast off right around their pilings or cleats on the dock and back on board to belay. Then when you want to cast off, just let go the end on the boat, haul on the other end, and, with any luck at all, you can haul the dock line right on board without the help of a linehandler ashore.

A word about fenders. Hang them in strategic spots, such as from lifeline stanchions (with a clove hitch backed by a half hitch as low on the stanchion as possible) or eye fittings on deck (with two half hitches). Hang fenders vertically. Reeve a half-inch line through the fender, tie a figure-eight knot in the end to stop it from coming back through, haul taut, and work another figure-eight knot into the long end of the fender line as close to the upper end of the fender as you can, so the line can't go back through the fender. Make your fender lines about six feet long, and whip the ends.

For lying up against a piling, have a fender board. This is simply a stout board, say a 2 x 6, about six feet long with a six-foot lanyard on each end (drill a hole, reeve the line

Getting underway. Notice which lines may be slack, and cast them off first (in this case, after spring). Visualize what will happen as you cast off each line. Letting go bow line will let her bow blow out a bit. Letting go forward spring will let her go forward a bit and let her bow out more. Then let go stern line, and she's underway.

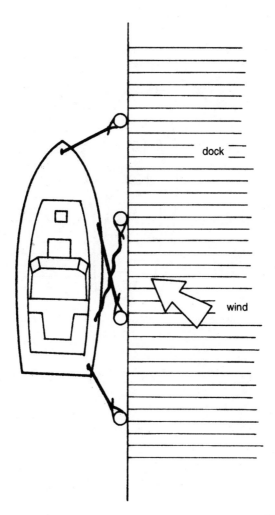

dock

wind

Getting underway. Backing against an after spring will throw the bow out against onsetting wind or current (or kicking ahead against a forward spring will throw the stern out).

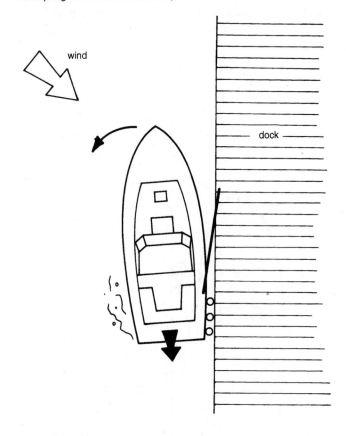

Landing. Get forward spring over and made down so you can use it to check headway and stop her in case your engine won't reverse.

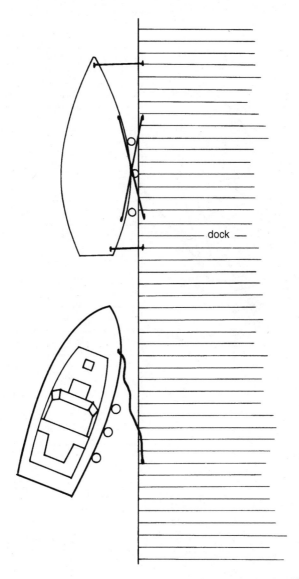

dock —

Landing. Back against after spring to bring her stern in.

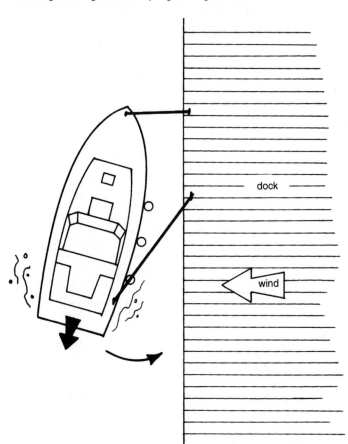

Landing. When single-handed, you may be able to tie up initially with just a short breast line amidships. Then take your time arranging other dock lines.

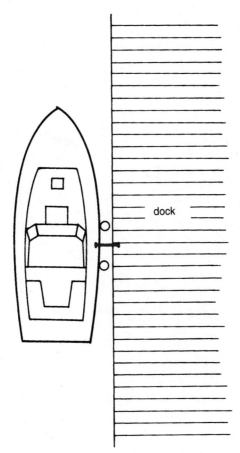

dock

Security. Lines 1–3 would be crucial (in that order) to holding her off the float to starboard. Double them up. Rig fenders to port as well as starboard in case your neighbor comes over for a midnight visit. Foward spring will take heaviest strain among starboard lines; double it.

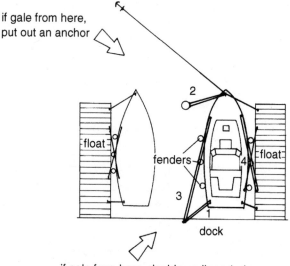

if gale from here, put out an anchor

float

fenders

float

2

4

3

1

dock

if gale from here, double up lines 1–4

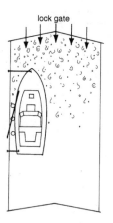

lock gate

Canal lock, going up (flooding). Crucial to hold bow line tight; don't let turbulence swing bow out, or you'll be sorry.

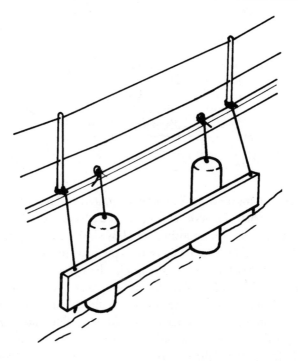

through, and tie in a figure-eight knot to stop it). Hang over two fenders, one on each side of the point where the piling would bear against the topsides, and then hang the board, tied to strong fittings with half the two fenders. By "strong fittings" I mean items such as deck fittings for lead blocks or chainplates. Don't tie to lifelines or high on lifeline stanchions; they might bend under the strain.

When tying up to a dock where there is a big range of tide, use long (five times the tidal range) lines for bow and stern lines (anchor rodes work well) and don't rig spring lines. The long bow and stern lines stretched way out ahead of and astern of the boat will keep her in the desired

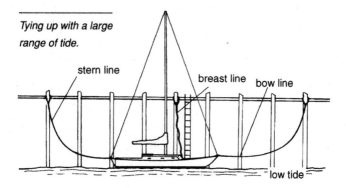

Tying up with a large range of tide.

stern line

breast line bow line

low tide

position fore and aft. You belay them so they'll be just slack at low water. Then rig a long (one and a half times the tidal range) breast line amidships and leave it slack at low water; this line gives you a way to pull the boat in to the dock from either the boat or the dock when you want to get ashore or back on board, for the long bow and stern lines won't necessarily hold her right in tight. Beware of projections on the boat or dock that could hang things up as the boat rises or falls. One sailor told me he woke up in the middle of the night at a Bay of Fundy dock with his vessel at a distinct angle and could only get her back on an even keel by operating on a dock timber with a chain saw.

Mooring Pendants

Sometimes you hold your boat on a permanent mooring, with a heavy rope mooring pendant ending in an eye splice that goes over a cleat or samson post. Make the mooring pendant of cable-laid nylon or polyester, twice as big as the anchor rode. Connect the pendant to the chain by splicing a tight eye around a thimble in the end of the pendant and shackling it to the chain.

Let's say you pick up your mooring, put the eye splice in the end of its pendant around your cleat or over your bitt or post, but then think, "What if she gets to pitching and surging on the pendant? Could that eye splice somehow come off the cleat or post?" Yes, it could. So you lash it, just in case. If the pendant is on a cleat, use a three-foot length of line, three turns of which will be as strong as the mooring pendant. Make a three-turn lashing round *one side* of the eye splice (the lashing goes *through* the eye) and the base of the cleat (the lashing goes through the hole in the base of the cleat). Then, if the eye somehow comes adrift, you will still have something as strong as the pendant holding your boat by the cleat. Occasionally you see a sailor put this lashing over both parts of the eye splice, but then the eye can simply pull right out from under the lashing. The lashing must go *through* the eye splice.

If the mooring pendant is on a post or bitt, a good way to lash it is with the end of an anchor rode. Make a bowline through the eye splice in mooring pendant, take the anchor rode to the other bitt or post, and make it fast as you normally would.

A nice rig is two separate mooring pendants. If one should somehow come adrift or chafe through in a gale, the other will hold the boat. If you rig two pendants, don't put eye splices in the inboard ends of them. It's almost impossible to make the splices so the two pendants will share the strain exactly evenly. Instead, just whip the ends. Then you can simply make each pendant fast to its post or cleat and adjust them to your heart's content. And you can change the point at which they go through the bow chocks so they won't always be wearing in the same place, "freshening the nip," as it's called. This last is also a reason to whip the end of a single mooring pendant rather than put an eye splice in it.

Towing

A special case of holding your boat is towing, when you need to hold her to a straining towline from another vessel. The basic guidelines for towing safety are to tow at reasonable speed and to accelerate very slowly. If you are the towed vessel, however, you may have little or no control over these matters, so you may have to cope with heavier strains than you'd like.

A towline will impart a lot more strain on a boat than her anchor line. For a tow of any duration in open water, the towline should be twice as heavy as the anchor line. If the towing vessel cannot provide a hawser of that size, your own anchor rode is the next best thing. For a short tow into the harbor in protected water, the anchor rode is perfectly adequate.

The towline should be as long as is reasonable, in order to gain elasticity. For our hypothetical 35-footer, 200 feet of towline would be about right in open water. A long towline dragging through the water does add a surprisingly large amount of resistance to the tow, but you need that length to reduce the impact of the sudden jerks when the towed and towing vessels get to pitching.

I prefer polyester to nylon for a towline. It would be good to have the elasticity of nylon, but all that stored-up energy can be dangerous if you need to slack or let go a heavily straining towline, or, especially, if it should part (see page 4). It's a dilemma: towing in heavy weather, you need all the elasticity you can get, but you certainly don't need the additional danger of potentially lethal energy on the stern of the towing vessel and bow of the towed vessel.

If you're the vessel being towed, make the towline fast as you would an anchor rode. The towboat hitch (naturally!) is ideal on a bitt or samson post. If you have only a heavy cleat for the anchor line, use it for the towline, putting on as many turns as the cleat will take. If you're worried about the line coming off the cleat, don't put a hitch on the last turn, but rather belay the line to some other convenient fitting, just to hold the last turn from coming off the cleat. In any case, make sure you can cast off the towline while it is under heavy strain, something you might need to do in an emergency.

If you have to take a towline from another vessel that is too big to go round any of your fittings, make an eye in the end of it with a bowline (with patience, you can form a bowline in even a relatively hefty hawser, two or three inches in diameter) and lash the eye to your anchor rode fitting as you would lash a mooring pendant, but with this vital difference: Don't put the eye over the fitting. Rather, depend entirely on the lashing to hold the towline. Again, this is so you can cast it off under strain if you have to.

If you doubt your fittings are strong enough to take the strain of a towline, you can use the mast to take some of the strain by simply leading the towline aft around the mast and then forward to belay as usual on the anchor rode fitting. Just the friction of the towline going 180 degrees around the mast will ease the strain on the fitting appreciably. *Never use this rig with a deck-stepped mast*, however, for the step is not designed to take a strong forward strain.

When your boat is doing the towing, obey the Golden Rule: Tow as you would be towed, easy and even. Make the towline fast to a strong fitting aft, such as a quarter bitt or heavy cleat, again in such a way that it may be cast off under strain. If you have heavy jibsheet winches, you can lead the towline around the winch and then aft to a quarter fitting, in the same way as you might use the mast forward.

Rather than towing from one quarter of the boat or the other, you may want to make a bridle leading to each quarter. This has the advantage of dividing the strain between two fittings and also makes steering easier. A good way to make a bridle is similar to putting a spring on your anchor rode. With, say, a 20-foot length of rope as heavy as the towline, tie a rolling hitch, backed by a half hitch, on the towline just outboard of the chock it leads through. Make the other end fast on the quarter fitting opposite the one where the towline is made fast (also in such a way that it can be cast off under strain). Then ease the towline until the strain on both lines is equal.

Whether towed or towing, you should lead towlines through chocks to reduce chafe. Whenever you are handling a towline, be extra careful and alert, because the line may come under sudden heavy strain. As with any heavily straining line, keep out of the line of fire as much as possible.

Towing a Dinghy

When towing a dinghy, add a towline to her painter by tying on with intersecting bowlines (see page 72) enough line to make up a total length of 100 feet. Make fast with a bowline a second 100-foot towline to a point on the dinghy other than the one where the painter is secured. Lead each towline through a chock on opposite

---

Towing a dinghy.

towlines secured as low as
practicable on dinghy's stem

quarters of the mother ship to belay; the slight angle between the towlines will help keep the dinghy from yawing, and if one line parts, you won't lose the boat. Secure the bitter end of each towline to its post or cleat with a bowline. The points of attachment on the dinghy should be as low to the water as possible, so she'll tow with her bow up. Sometimes a beach "pebble" in the stern helps, too. You don't always have to tow the dinghy 100 feet astern, of course, but at times, as in a rough following sea, you'll want all that towline out so the dinghy can't hit your stern when she comes charging at you down the face of a wave.

Chafing Gear

Chafe is a concern with any anchor rode, mooring pendant, dock line, or towline. If any of these lines comes under heavy strain, it may well chafe—even where it passes through smooth chocks. And if it has to pass over or around any comparatively sharp object, such as a rail or the bobstay under a bowsprit, it will certainly chafe. The best protection is chafing gear, secured to the line at the probable point of chafe. A good kind of chafing gear is rubber or plastic hose, split lengthwise to fit around the rope. Make the hose about two feet long and put a hole in each end to take lanyards of small stuff. Tie each lanyard (about a foot long) into its hole with a buntline hitch, and tie each lanyard around the rope with a rolling hitch to hold the chafing gear in place. Alternatively, you can use heavy strips of canvas wrapped diagonally around the rope with each end lashed securely (beyond the area of chafe) with small stuff. To lash canvas chafing gear, just make a clove hitch around the wrapped rope, pull it up hard, and add a good, snug half hitch.

17 Keeping Gear from Getting Adrift

Securing Gear on Deck

It's always disconcerting, when the boat begins to heel and roll and pitch and the lee deck goes occasionally awash, to have the boathook wash overboard, a coiled halyard fall off its cleat in a tangle, and the ship's radio dive off its shelf onto the chart table with a crash. So a good rule when getting underway is to assume it will soon be rough, if it isn't already, and to lash down everything that could go adrift.

On deck, the most important things to lash down are the anchors. The last thing you need in a seaway is heavy anchors banging about the bow. Some anchors have metal fittings with removable pins to hold them securely in place. Otherwise, you can lash the anchors down with something heavier than small stuff, ¼-inch rope at the least. Lash to something heavy, a post, bitt, or cleat for the anchor rode, a mast or bowsprit, or to an eyebolt through the deck, put in just for the purpose. Take at least three turns around what you are lashing to and the part of the anchor you are lashing. Put separate lashings on ring and flukes. Snug each turn up taut and finish off by putting three half hitches round all the turns together. Putting the half hitches round all the turns hauls them tightly together and pulls the lashing really taut. Or, fin-

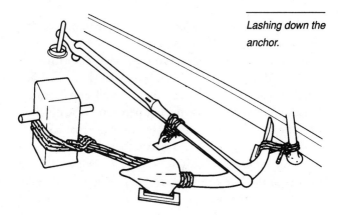

ish off with a clove hitch round either the fitting or the
anchor and add a half hitch. Take pride in making these
lashings tight and neat. Visualize forces coming on your
lashings from all different directions and make sure the
anchor can't come loose. If, say, your lashings are fine from
all directions but one, figure out an additional lashing that
will hold the anchor in that direction also. Lashings can be
quite creative.

The Dinghy

The dinghy is usually lashed upside down. That way
it offers less resistance to wave and wind, can't fill with
water, and won't be attractive as a catch-all for gear better
stowed more securely elsewhere. Lash each end of the
dinghy to something strong. (The "something strong"
applies, of course, as much to the fittings on the dinghy
as to the fittings on the boat that carries her.) Again, use
several turns of at least ¼-inch line, haul taut each turn
evenly, and finish off with half hitches round all the turns,
or a clove hitch and half hitch. In addition, run a line up
over the dinghy's hull, athwartship at each end and diago-

nally both ways across the bottom, using handrails on the cabin house or other fittings on deck, whatever is convenient, to run the line through on the boat. Start this line with a buntline hitch on the first fitting, cinch up very taut each part that goes up over the dinghy's hull, and finish off with a rolling hitch tied to the last part across the dinghy's hull. The rolling hitch will enable you to get that last part tied as tightly as you cinched it. Another good way to finish off the dinghy hull lashing is to tie a bowline into the last part of the line coming across the dinghy's hull, take the end through your last cabin-top or deck fitting, go back up through the bowline, and then haul on it harder than you can, using the bowline as a makeshift purchase giving you a two-to-one mechanical advantage. Finish off with two, or preferably, three, half hitches right at the bowline. This method will make the dinghy hull lashing really taut. A heavy strain can come on the dinghy lashings if a sea breaks on the little boat, for even upside down, her hull will offer a lot of resistance to all that heavy water moving fast.

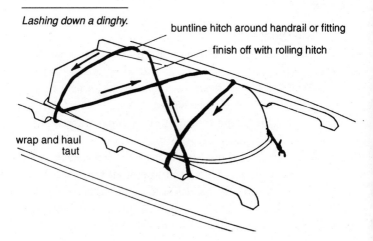

Lashing down a dinghy.

buntline hitch around handrail or fitting

finish off with rolling hitch

wrap and haul taut

Miscellaneous Gear

Lashing down other, lighter-weight gear on deck, such as the boathook, spinnaker pole, deck swab, awning, dinghy oars, or what-have-you, can be done with small stuff. I prefer small-diameter, braided polyester for this work. Have a big hank of it always handy; you can't have too much. When you cut off a piece for a new lashing you thought up, the ends of this stuff seem to stay in place, and you can get away without whipping them. Lash both ends of whatever it is you are keeping from going adrift; use plenty of turns (at least three), and finish off with half hitches round the turns or a clove hitch and a half hitch. When lashing things down, remember to be sure that any running rigging in the vicinity is left free and clear. It's embarrassing to tack and find you just lashed the weather jib sheet in with the spinnaker pole.

If you're expecting really heavy weather, send below everything you reasonably can, and double up on the lashings of everything movable that must stay on deck.

Securing Items Below

Now, let's go below and make the cabin ready for sea. Visualize the boat knocked way down on first one side and then the other, and secure everything movable so nothing can get loose on either of these knockdowns. Throw in some violent pitching for good measure. Again, that big hank of small-diameter, braided polyester will be the thing to use to secure gear. If any piece of electronics gear isn't permanently mounted—for instance, a broadcast radio used chiefly for entertainment—lash it in place. Put in screw eyes for fittings to lash to, if nothing else makes a convenient lashing point. As usual, give your lashings at least three turns, and finish off with half

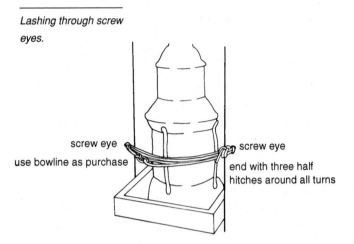

Lashing through screw eyes.

screw eye

use bowline as purchase

screw eye

end with three half hitches around all turns

hitches round all parts, three half hitches being better than two. Alternatively, make a small bowline in the end of your lashing line, reeve the other end through the screw eye, and pull the line through the screw eye until the bowline is almost at the screw eye. Then pass the lashing round the object you are securing, reeve the end through the bowline and haul taut, using the bowline as a purchase, an easy way to make the first turn really tight. Then add the rest of your turns through the screw eye, hauling each as taut as possible, and finish off with half hitches round all the turns.

Small sticks and wedges, perhaps combed from the beaches you cruise to, are handy for securing gear below. They can be used to wedge tightly into place items such as the alcohol stove atop the solid-fuel stove, books on a shelf, or a water canister in a cockpit locker. When using this dunnage, the geometric creativity of the cargo stower comes into play. And if you can't get a lashing as tight as you'd really like, you can always put a wedge under it to tighten it up.

If fragile gear is stowed in net hammocks or in hanging bags, the hammocks and bags need to be lashed so they won't bang against the ceiling or bulkhead. One turn around the middle of the hammock or bag hauled taut to a screw eye ought to suffice. The same sort of restrainer is good for keeping the clothes hanging in a locker from rubbing back and forth with every roll, wearing themselves out on a long passage. A good way to tie off such a restraining lashing is to make a half hitch and not pull the end through, so you have a bight of line left. This won't jam and can be untied simply by pulling on the end of the line. Finish off by tying the second half hitch with the bight. Being doubled (by using the bight), the half hitch will be easier to untie than one with a single part. This way of tying half hitches loses a bit in security but gains in quickness of untying, so it's good for restrainers that you may want to let go frequently.

18 Handling Weight

Going Aloft

Sooner or later every sailor needs to go aloft to do a bit of rigging work, replace a lightbulb, retrieve a lost halyard, or simply inspect his rig. The force of gravity being what it is, some safety precautions are in order.

First of all, going aloft is normally a two-person operation, one to go aloft and the other to do the hoisting. The sailor going aloft should dress for protection with non-skid shoes, long pants, and a long-sleeved shirt. He or she might slip and have to hang on, so the fewer scrapes and scratches the better.

Inspect your boatswain's chair before you trust your life to it. The canvas sling type of boatswain's chair is certainly more comfortable than the wooden swing type, and you're less likely to fall out of it. Using the biggest shackle that will fit, secure the boatswain's chair to the halyard that has the most purchase and will take you where you want to go. Lead that halyard to your best winch, which may well mean through a lead block to the anchor windlass. The winch operator must work carefully and unhurriedly. He should keep his ears open for instructions from on high and should send reassuring acknowledgments of those instructions back up the mast. Occasionally, the winch operator may have to look

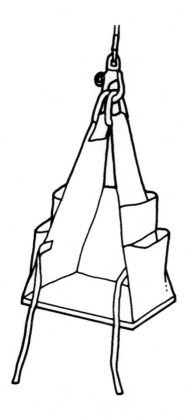

Canvas boatswain's chair.

up at the sailor aloft to see what's going on, but anytime he is hoisting or lowering, his eyes should be on his work. When lowering a sailor down a mast, keep three turns on winch or cleat and lower as steadily and smoothly as you can.

I always hate to see sailors going aloft on just one halyard. For both convenience and safety, shackle into the boatswain's chair a second, separate halyard. That way the sailor going aloft can assist in the hoisting, or at least follow up closely on the hoisting, by grasping the second halyard and hauling away on it. And if something goes wrong with the first halyard, he'll have some options. He

Second halyard on a boatswain's chair.

sailor going aloft can assist in the hoisting

can support his own weight on the second halyard and can lower himself back down to a spreader or to the deck. (He'll thank his lucky stars if the halyard has purchase.) Or, his helpmate on deck can take the second halyard to a winch or cleat and lower him.

If the best halyard to go aloft on happens to be a wire one leading to a reel winch, you have the special problem of what to do about releasing the brake of the winch when it's time for the sailor aloft to come down. The winch operator who releases the brake may or may not be able to control the sailor's weight with the winch handle (see page 36). This is where that second halyard is essential. It can be belayed, and the sailor aloft can take his own weight on it while the brake is released. Then both halyards can be eased together.

Hoisting Heavy Loads with Halyards

In addition to people going aloft there are other types of heavy loads that sometimes need to be lifted and moved around on boats. It's a good idea in any cruising boat, for example, to carry a really heavy anchor, two to three times as heavy as her normal anchors, for that gale that may catch her in other than ideal anchoring conditions or to give her half a chance of hanging on in a heavy storm. Here's a good alternative to manhandling an anchor of, say, 50 pounds or more out over the bow when you want to get it ready to let go, and back in again after you've weighed it. Handle it with a headsail halyard. Let's hope your headsail halyard has a two-part purchase, as described in Chapter 11. If it doesn't, you presumably have a winch to supply the mechanical advantage you need. Shackle the halyard into the ring of the anchor and hoist away carefully, guiding the anchor so it doesn't hit anything. When you have the anchor high enough to clear the rail or lifelines, push it out over the water, hold it out away from the boat, and lower it to the water's edge, until it takes its weight on the rode. Unshackle the halyard. This is a lot easier and more controlled than manhandling. The operation is easiest with two people, one to hoist and one to guide the anchor. You can, however, hoist the anchor by yourself with a two-part halyard. Take the hauling part of the halyard to where you need to be on the deck to guide the anchor. Use one hand to hoist and the other to guide. To get a new grip on the halyard to hoist again, hold everything steady with the guiding hand by grasping both parts of the halyard leading from the block and squeezing them together just above the lower block of the halyard. This will hold the anchor up where you hoisted it and steady it at the same time. You'll find you can hold a lot of weight with one hand this way. If you have to use a winch for power, then you'll need to have two people. When weighing anchor, simply reverse the process.

In a similar way, you can hoist on board heavy objects, such as a man overboard, a new heating stove, or a barrel of rum, using the main halyard and a cargo sling. If you

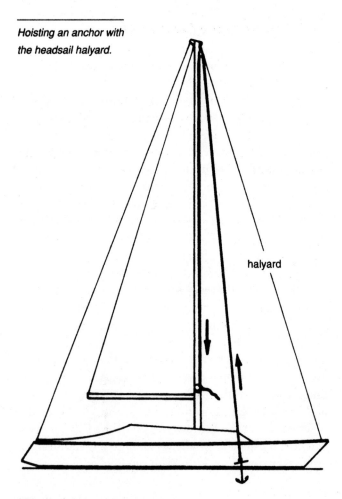

Hoisting an anchor with the headsail halyard.

halyard

don't have a ready-made cargo sling, a good makeshift one for the man overboard is the boatswain's chair. For other loads, use a stout line to go around each end of the cargo so it will balance, take enough turns so it won't slip, then come up through the shackle on the halyard block, tying off with half hitches.

Hoisting with the Main Boom

If you need to hoist on board something that's too heavy to be guided by hand on the main halyard, such as a heavy dinghy, a good way to do it—if you have a topping lift and a sheet with adequate purchase—is to use the main boom as a cargo boom. Unshackle the lower sheet block or blocks, and shackle them to the cargo sling. Rig your preventer on the boom to hold the boom outboard at the desired angle (see page 118). And rig a second "preventer" to the end of the boom simply leading inboard to belay, so you can swing the boom in (slacking the forward preventer, of course).

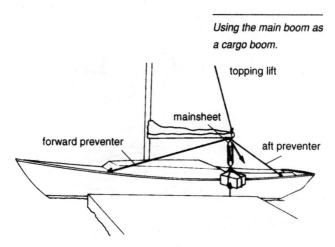

Using the main boom as a cargo boom.

topping lift

mainsheet

forward preventer

aft preventer

Now you are ready to operate your cargo boom. Heave in on the topping lift to raise the boom high enough so the cargo will clear the rail or lifelines when the sheet is two-blocked. Set the boom at the desired angle to the boat's centerline with the two preventers. Use the mainsheet winch if you have one, or lead the sheet forward along the boom to a mast winch, and heave away to lift the cargo high enough to clear everything when you swing it inboard. Swing the boom in, heaving on one preventer and slacking the other. When the cargo is positioned where you want it, lower away carefully with the sheet.

Hoisting with Davits

A great luxury is to have a boat big enough for boat davits, so you can hoist your dinghy up astern or, better yet, up outboard amidships to be swung in on deck. Even a small dinghy weighs a lot, so have at least a four-part purchase on the davit falls (double lower block); if the small boat

---

"Griping her in against a pudding."

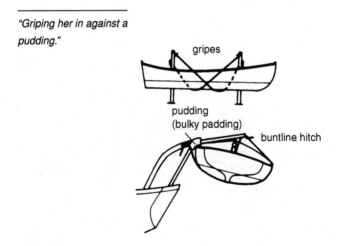

gripes

pudding
(bulky padding)

buntline hitch

weighs over 200 pounds, go to six parts (triple lower block). Make it a pleasure to hoist out or lower away your boat. If the boat is to hang outboard, it's best to "gripe her in against a pudding," as old-timers would say. The pudding is simply a heavy, bulky piece of padding secured where the inboard side of the hoisted boat will bear against it (perhaps on a pole between the davits). The gripes are single-part, diagonal lashings run right round the small boat and hauled taut to keep her from swinging. Dead-end a gripe at an eye fitting on the davit head with a buntline hitch, run it diagonally under the small boat, and haul taut, belaying to a cleat on the other davit. The gripes not only keep the small boat from swinging, but also act as preventers to keep her from falling should the falls be inadvertently let go or come unhooked.

19   Safety Gear and Operations

The second biggest disaster at sea (the first, surely, being sinking) is to lose a sailor overboard. Rope can be used both to prevent and to recover from this catastrophe.

At sea, it's a good idea to rig temporary, heavy rope lifelines at strategic points around the boat. Determine where the best place is to tie high lifelines, say a couple of feet above your permanent lifelines, maybe stretched from headstay to shrouds and then back to a gallows frame or backstay. On a flush-decked boat, you may want to set up a lifeline right along the centerline. A boat I was on recently has a wide, high main cabin fully capable of cracking ribs, or worse, when she takes a sudden lurch, so the crew set up a temporary lifeline below when at sea.

Temporary lifelines are a good chance for rigging creativity. Dead-end with a buntline hitch, reeve the other end through or around its fitting, and tie in a small bowline about three feet short of the fitting. Reeve the end through the bowline, haul really taut on that simple purchase, and tie off with half hitches at the bowline.

A safety harness, a strong web buckled tightly about the upper body, can keep you from falling overboard. It has a very strong, short lanyard leading from the buckle in front, ending in a carabiner-type clip. You clip this lanyard into or around strong fittings to tether yourself

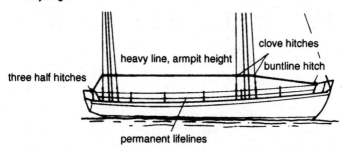

Rigging a temporary lifeline. Work from forward to aft, setting up taut as you go.

clove hitches

heavy line, armpit height

buntline hitch

three half hitches

permanent lifelines

should you lose your balance. A good rig is a wire leading along the deck on each side of the boat, at deck level, shackled into a strong fitting at each end, that lets you clip on before leaving the cockpit and go all the way to the bow without unclipping.

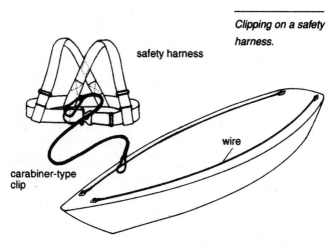

Clipping on a safety harness.

safety harness

carabiner-type clip

wire

The line that can help you recover a sailor lost overboard is a 100-foot piece of half-inch rope with rescue gear (see below) and floats on it that you can trail over the stern. Such a line will greatly increase the chance of maneuvering *something* within the person's grasp, so you can get him or her back on board.

This lifeline is a good use for polypropylene, because it floats. The more fluorescent the color, the better. Along the line, say every 25 feet, put on a small float, painted fluorescent orange. Secure each float by reeving the line through it and tying a figure eight knot snug up against each of its sides.

On the end that is to go overboard, have the best lifesaving device you can get. The Lifesling is a good choice. It's a strong, floating belt, secured to a line with an eye splice. The sailor in the water, if not disabled, puts the sling around his or her body under the arms and can then be pulled back to the boat and hauled on board. Other choices would be a life jacket, life ring, or boatswain's chair tied on with a bowline. The inboard end of the line should be kept belayed to a strong fitting on the stern with a bowline. To stow the line so it will run free when needed, fake it carefully into a deck bucket lashed upright on the stern, say to the stern pulpit. (Faking is described on page 48.)

When cruising coastwise, towing a dinghy with a long towline in reserve provides a similar safety line for a sailor overboard.

Hauling a person back on board can be difficult, of course, particularly if the person is unable to help. If the adrenalin of the rescuer or rescuers is not enough to simply haul the person over the rail and lifelines, one of the ways of handling weight described in the previous chapter may prove useful. The biggest dangers in using one of these methods are the time it would take to prepare such a rig and the difficulty of keeping the person suspended by

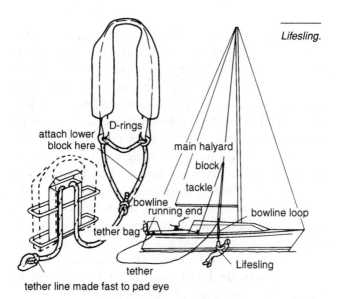

attach lower block here

D-rings

main halyard

block

tackle

bowline

running end

bowline loop

tether bag

tether

Lifesling

tether line made fast to pad eye

halyard or boom from swinging when the boat rolls. To keep the person from swinging outboard and then back against the boat, rig a separate line around the hoisting line to the person, down near the point of attachment of the hoisting line. Belay one end of this line to a stout fitting on deck, and tend the other end.

The Lead Line

An essential piece of line in a boat is the lead line. If you have a fathometer, that's well and good, but someday it may be out of batteries or have some more serious sickness. The lead line will always tell you how deep the water is, and, if you keep the hollow in the bottom of the lead well armed with grease, it may even tell you something of the nature of the bottom.

It's not a bad idea to have two lead lines—a long, heavy one for work in relatively deep water, say from three fathoms to 30 fathoms, and a short, light one, three fathoms long. For the long one, use ¼-inch rope, get a standard lead made for the purpose, and mark the lead at standard intervals. For the short one, use cod fishing line with a cod fishing sinker. Mark the line at one, two, and three fathoms simply by tying one, two, and three overhand knots at those points in the line. Make the line long enough so that the three-fathom mark will reach the water's edge when you are holding the line from a standing position on deck. Now you're ready to take soundings in deep water with your big lead line and very quickly in shoal water with your little one, whether or not your fathometer is belly up. Don't forget to tie the bitter end of the lead line around something with a bowline.

Well, I hope you've had fun with all these knots and blocks and reevings. Once you get into it, rigging up all this stuff can be most satisfying. These basic hints should give you a start in working up a lot of your own variations and pet ways of doing things. Here's wishing you big blocks and small ropes!

Bibliography

Ashley, Clifford W. *The Ashley Book of Knots.* New York: Doubleday, 1944. Perhaps the most incredible fact about this book is that it took Ashley only eleven years to write and illustrate it. This is the *Oxford English Dictionary* (unabridged) of traditional ropework.

Graumont, Raoul, and John Hensel. *The Encyclopedia of Knots and Fancy Ropework*, 4th ed. Cambridge, Maryland: Cornell Maritime Press, 1952. If you can't find it in here, it probably isn't worth looking for.

Henderson, Richard. *Understanding Rigs and Rigging.* Rev. ed. Camden, Maine: International Marine, 1991. Objective discussion of modern rigs with an excellent chapter on running rigging and related fittings.

Jarman, Colin. *The Essential Knot Book.* Camden, Maine: International Marine, 1985. A quick explanation of 27 knots, 4 whippings, and 12 splices.

Norgrove, Ross. *Cruising Rigs and Rigging.* Camden, Maine: International Marine, 1982. Includes excellent advice on ways to use rope and to set up a sound rig for cruising offshore.

Porter, Daniel. "Knowing the Ropes." *WoodenBoat* 109 (1992): 72–79. An illuminating technical discussion of rope materials and construction, including coverage of recently developed ropes that are extremely strong, resistant to stretch, and expensive.

Toss, Brion. *The Rigger's Apprentice.* 2d ed. Camden, Maine: International Marine, 1992. A professional rigger shares his hard-won tricks of the trade.

—. *The Rigger's Locker: Tools and Techniques for Modern and Traditional Rigging.* Camden, Maine: International Marine, 1992. A fine sequel to *The Rigger's Apprentice.*

Index

The Rigger's Apprentice, Second Edition
Brion Toss
Illustrated by Robert Shetterly
The Rigger's Apprentice is not just another knot book, even though the knots a sailor needs are all here. Nor is it a survey of rigs, for the subject is rigging itself: its principles and procedures.
"A masterpiece on the subject of rigging."—*Sailing*
Paperbound, 208 pages, 600 illustrations, $22.95.
Order No. 60360P.

The Nature of Boats: Insights and Esoterica for the Nautically Obsessed

Dave Gerr

The Nature of Boats is the ideal companion for old salts, boatyard crawlers, boatshow oglers, and landlocked dreamers. It's packed with understandable explanations of the difference between initial and reserve stability, of how torque and horsepower work, of traditional boat-building materials versus high-tech, of rudder control, of speed powered by sails versus engines, of flotation and trim. Dave Gerr examines sail and power boats from every conceivable angle to create a book that's not only fascinating and fun, but also extremely useful.

"Fascinating potpourri of information about today's boats, modern and traditional; reminiscent of the work of Culler, Lane, Davis, Atkin, and many others of an earlier era."—*WoodenBoat*

"Gerr understands those of us afflicted with a passion for boats. Furthermore he trades on our insatiable appetites for nautical tidbits. And he does it well. Gerr has a talent for describing complicated concepts in simple terms."—*SEA*

Hardbound, 432 pages, 253 illustrations, $29.95.
Order No. 60262H.

Boat Trailers and Tow Vehicles: A User's Guide
Steve Henkel

Densely illustrated with Steve Henkel's clear drawings, this book is packed with information showing adjustment, towing, launching, maintenance, and repair procedures. It describes how to choose the right style and type of trailer for a particular boat and trailering venue; how to choose the best tow vehicle; how to troubleshoot and repair the electrics and wheel bearings; how to correct sway and stability problems while towing; and much more. Detailed appendices include trailer towing regulations by state; trailer towing ratings for cars, vans, and pickups; and a product source list.

"A book like this has been long needed.... [It covers] subjects that often take boaters several years to learn. It's a good investment."—*Trailer Boats*

"The best single source guide I've seen. Commonsense advice, and nicely organized."—*American Sailor*

"A no-fluff practical primer that can help the trailer boater steer a safe course along the highways to the high seas."—*Sailing*

Paperbound, 144 pages, 50 illustrations, $14.95.
Order No. 60264P.

Gently with the Tides: The Best of *Living Aboard*

Edited by Michael Frankel

Fueled by 17 years of the best letters, articles, and first-hand accounts from *Living Aboard* journal, *Gently with the Tides* is a powerful testimonial to the lure and romance of living aboard a boat. Most of all, it's a high-octane dream-feeder for liveaboard aspirants. It will help them decide whether to, it will tell them how to, and, most important, it will fill their dreams with why to.

Paperbound, 256 pages, 16 illustrations, $14.95.

Order No. 60374P.

**Look for These and Other International Marine Books at Your
Local Bookstore**

To order, call toll free: 1-800-822-8158
(outside the U.S., call 717-794-2191)
or write to: International Marine/TAB Books,
A Division of McGraw-Hill, Inc.
Blue Ridge Summit, PA 17294-0840.

Title	Product No.	Quantity	Price

Subtotal: $_____

Postage and Handling
($3.00 in U.S., $5.00 outside U.S.): $_____

Add applicable state and local sales tax: $_____

TOTAL: $_____

❑ Check or money order made payable to TAB Books

Charge my: ❑ VISA ❑ MasterCard ❑ American Express

Acct. No.: _____ Exp.: _____

Signature: _____

Name: _____

Address: _____

City: _____

State: _____ Zip: _____

Orders outside U.S. must pay with international money order in U.S.
dollars. If for any reason you are not satisfied with the book(s) you
order, simply return it (them) within 15 days and receive a
full refund.